WSW 85

Stories and Poems from
West Sussex Writers

2022

Copyright

Edited by Phil Williams
Cover art © Audrey Lee
Published by Rumian Publishing

ISBN: 978-1-913468-22-4

Dedicated to Ian Black
West Sussex Writers Chairman
2016 - 2022

CONTENTS

PART ONE - PROSE

PART TWO - POETRY

PART ONE

PROSE

Four Friends

Lawrence Long

This piece is to celebrate four good friends of mine, members of West Sussex Writers, who have now gone to the great writing workshop in the sky.

IAN MALLENDER was a WSW stalwart, particularly involved in the organisation of several Days For Writers. This involved liaison with Northbrook College, our then venue, which was not always easy. Such as the time Ian and team (including me) turned up on the Saturday concerned to find that, with no word to us, the man with whom we had made all arrangements had suddenly been suspended for reasons unspecified, and others knew little about our Day. That it still ran smoothly was a tribute to Ian's diplomatic skills. Sadly he would later succumb to Parkinson's.

Ian had behind him a successful business career with spells in Japan and the US, the latter leaving him with an attractive mid-Atlantic accent. He was always full of good humour including in his short stories such as "Wood-Eye" (pun intended). He also saved his local The Gun Inn, Findon, from closure. For some of us inland writers, this was a watering stop on the way home from WSW. A fine moment from an early Saturday when I gave him a lift to the Day For Writers. Then, the late great Brian Matthew hosted "Sounds of the Sixties" at 8 a.m. on Saturdays. The old hit "Do You Know The Way To San José?" came on.

Ian: "Yes, I used to live there."

PETA SANDARS (aka Jane Gurney) was the first person I ever met at WSW. It was at Day For Writers 1994 and she was a designated meeter-and-greeter. She did so well that I joined, was later Chairman and am still in it today. She was very friendly, some of which may have been relief at being up and about after a hospital stay with the MS she already had. Tall, willowy and auburn-haired, she had many writing credits and was keen enough to drive from Farnham, Surrey, for meetings in Worthing. Her most successful book, as Jane Gurney (two of her real names) was

The Green of the Spring, a First World War novel covering both the men in the trenches and the women back home: 50,000 sold, 60,000 library borrowings (also remunerative). The follow up, delivered late, was less successful, but she wrote much, including songs (she played guitar and sang in folk clubs), humorous ballads, a novella, *Paris Fever,* for fans of that city, and the lyrics for a musical *Woman*, a success at the Edinburgh Fringe. She is much missed.

LEONIE MANSELL was a performance poet of feminist and socialist persuasion who will be remembered by anyone who saw her perform. Refusing to go gently, she kept her hair red and learned her poems by heart. She once came second in the WSW Poetry Competition under controversial circumstances when she was marked down for using a nursery rhyme as basis for satire. She had won poetry competitions on the page in St Albans (Ver Poets) and Bournemouth (The Russell Coates Cup). A member of several small performing groups in her native London (a true Cockney, despite the Staffs accent from her childhood there) and Sussex. She had started with Brentford Poets. She passed on in 2021.

VIRGINIA MONSON was perhaps less involved with WSW but was a sometime member. She had been a journalist by profession since leaving school, although she didn't have the qualifications then required. She worked in this role in East Grinstead, Brighton and Lancashire. After retirement, she took to poetry at which, with her word skills, she unsurprisingly excelled. She was a member of several groups in Sussex and took part in several courses in Sussex and Kent. Petite and dynamic, she was a good friend of other Brighton-based poets such as Fay Marshall and Finola Holiday. Virginia passed on in summer 2022.

A Cissbury Dream

Norman Allcorn

Sometimes things happen to you that you know are very unlikely to occur again. A combination of time, place and event, like seeing a total eclipse, or the return of a comet.

Such a thing happened to me a number of years ago.

It was a misty morning in early Autumn and I was late in taking my dogs for a walk. In fact it was nearly lunchtime, which was unusual in itself as I almost always went out very early.

I liked to put my two collie dogs in the car and drive to the small car park above Nepcote. I liked to walk through the flint mines, enjoy the solitude, and look over a sleeping Worthing. To the west was Highdown, and if it was a clear day, you could see the Isle of Wight, like a small wedge of cheese in the distance. Further round the ring, to the east, was the scar of the cement works at Shoreham, and then Brighton and the Seven Sisters. To the north was Chanctonbury Ring, and to the south, the silver sea.

On this particular day, though, no views were possible due to the fog.

I ascended Cissbury by the steep path and went round the ring anti-clockwise. There was that feeling of isolation that one gets when walking in very poor visibility. Familiar objects near to you look strange, and those in the distance look totally foreign. The sun was trying to break through from above, but at ground level the fog was persisting. I reached the far side of the ring and started to descend by the lower of the two diagonal tracks. There was a tractor working below but I couldn't see it. Then it stopped, and soon, out the mist came a huge flock of seagulls, hundreds if not thousands of them, of all sizes, from the small black-headed gulls to the large herring gulls. They flew around me in a great aerial ballet, gliding effortlessly on the wind. They all seemed oblivious to me and my dogs. I stood and watched them for several minutes, entranced by this display. Even their normal raucous calling was dulled by the mist to a gentle, musical, mewing. As they flew around me it was as almost if I was part of the flock. Almost as if I could have spread my arms and joined them.

5

Then, just as suddenly as it started, the spell was broken. Most of the flock flew off towards Chanctonbury but some went over Findon and Church Hill. As I returned to the car park, the sun had burnt off the remaining mist, and I could see below me a brown, fully ploughed field with a few white blobs. These were a few stragglers still searching the newly turned earth for worms or grubs. The main flock were now just black dots in the distance, leaving me to wonder if it had really happened. It certainly had been a dreamlike experience and one that I was not likely to witness again. However, I knew that it was real, and that I would never forget it.

Not a Common Bird

Audrey Lee

(A real event of forty-five years ago)

"Mum, mum! Come and see, quick!"

I ran out into the road from where my children were calling excitedly, drying my hands on a tea towel. What greeted me was a dilemma.

I live near the sea, and enormous white sea birds are always circling overhead, wheeling and screeching in their appointed place. This one offended the laws of nature, for it was sitting squarely in the middle of the road like the centrepiece of a Surrealist painting, bristling its wings and hissing like a goose. Out of the sky, seagulls are big, amazingly big. This one was the size of a large cat. And it was white, a brilliant Persil white, whiter than that. Its wings beat with enormous strength, nearly but not quite lifting the heavy body. Then we saw the cruel gash of blood under one wing.

"Mum! What can we do?"

I had to do something, but what? I'm not a great interferer in nature, on the whole. I have always felt that to throw my paltry bit of pity into its bloody grinding machine is a bit pointless. I've never chased the cat to retrieve the squeaking things it caught or revived a fallen sparrow with drops of water from a syringe, but this was different. The situation was critical. We lived in a quiet residential area and very little traffic came down our road, but even if a dog or cat came along there might be carnage.

"Quick, run to the corner shop and get a cardboard box – the bigger the better."

I thought it would be a simple matter to drop this box over the bird and scoop it up inside. It wasn't simple. The box swelled under our hands, shuffling and lurching with the living thing inside it, threatening to burst at the seams. What could I do? With difficulty I took the heavy seething mass into the house and placed it in the best place I could think of: our downstairs cloakroom,

7

bigger than a cupboard, smaller than a room. I managed to get it in and shut the door.

It was then that my surreal scene became really disturbing, for the bird went absolutely mad, throwing its wounded body about in a frenzy, beating against the door, uttering shrill staccato shrieks, and it suddenly dawned on me that I had sinned against nature. I had put a wild and inhuman creature into an environment as alien to it as Mars would be to me. Was the fear I had inflicted on it any less awful than the death it would have met on the road? We were all upset. Our instinct was to calm the bird, to comfort it, but we realised at once that no comfort was possible. Our voices were human, our arms were not wings.

When it had quietened of its own accord I opened the door a crack and peeped in. The bird was standing on the ruins of the box, backed into a corner, facing the door. It fixed me with a stare so wild and strange that I was suddenly acutely aware of the utter incongruity of my own flesh and blood, and how it circumscribed my experience of life. What was it like to live in that bird's body, to wheel and dive through the air, to live by instinct alone without logic or reason? Did the bird feel free as we feel free when it soared on a rising current of air, and did it now feel imprisoned as we would feel imprisoned? Did it, bereft of speech and mental calculation, actually feel far more intensely than we do ourselves? I wondered, in that moment of time, whether the bird's mode of being was actually superior to my own, that it might have felt more joy, more pleasure, more excitement, than I who was so often ground down by the boredom of life, and I felt a brief but clearly identifiable humiliation. Or perhaps it was simply an echo of that age-old envy that all earth bound creatures feel for the faculty of flight? I thought all these things in an instant, in the moment it took to open the door an inch, and close it again.

In the end, my dilemma was solved by a miraculous Mrs Barlow who, the police informed me, devoted her life to the care of wild birds and had a hundred of them in her house at any one time. She descended on us like an archetypal District Nurse, all practicality and confidence. Feathers and beak were quelled with expert skill; in fact, after the initial flurry, the bird sank into the box she had brought with what sounded to me like an unnecessarily grateful squawk. In her opinion, it had probably been hit by a car, but with special care she might be able to release it after a few days. She was a great hit with the children who watched her with awe and fascination and played at being Mrs

Barlows for several weeks after.

Mrs Barlow pronounced the bird to be a Common Gull, which is not a common bird. As my daughter remarked, sitting on the front doorstep afterwards, it was probably the most uncommon bird in the world.

My inadequacy with this representative of the feathered species, and with Mrs Barlow, left me feeling somewhat diminished. I was glad when they had left the house and I could shake off what I had glimpsed in that bird's blank and beady eye.

All this happened nearly fifty years ago now, and the children have grown up and gone. I still live with my husband in the same house, but it and practically everything else around it has changed. The houses and garages have changed, the neighbours have changed umpteen times and the street has changed from being empty to one where cars are parked nose to tail on either side. The greatest change is in my garden, which has become a veritable jungle teeming with suburban wildlife. We used to whoop with delight at the occasional hedgehog, now we can sit at the window and see squirrels darting from tree to tree, a family of foxes playing under our shed, magpies, pigeons and crows vying with each other for whatever they can find, the delightful flurries of sparrows and thrush across the lawn – and, of course, seagulls.

My relationship with seagulls has changed completely. I no long philosophise when confronted at close quarters with a seagull. Now I am more likely to brandish the broom and shoo it away.

You can see seagulls everywhere, nesting on the roofs around, struggling to feed a crop of hungry mouths, and it is difficult not to throw them a slice of stale bread (we have even buttered it). It is also great fun to throw out a handful of food and enjoy the ensuing maelstrom of beaks and feathers. But their persistent squawking and clamouring for food has become a nuisance and they are becoming quite fearless.

Today I was sitting on the sofa when a seagull walked into my house, flew at the curtains and pooped all over the hearthrug. I charged at it with the kitchen mop and gave it what for. I am pleased to say that this time the confrontation, fifty years after the first one, did not leave me feeling inadequate.

Oranges Put a Smile on Her Face

Rose Bray

"Janet, my dear, I have some good news for you." He fiddled with the top button of his waistcoat as he talked.

"What is it, James?" Janet's heart did a nervous flip. She carried on dusting the shelves of their shop ready to replace the canisters. Whenever he approached her in that tone of voice with his blue eyes sliding sideways, she began to feel worried.

"I got an absolute bargain today!" he said.

Oh no, she thought, remembering the sack of flour he'd bought last year from a travelling miller. That had been a bargain as well. It had been full of flour mites which she only noticed when the flour began walking across the floor of the shop. They'd had to give the whole sack to Andy McBride for his pigs.

"Well, you know the boat that's been sheltering in the harbour?" He cleared his throat.

"Yes," she said, glancing out of the window where she could just see the tips of the tall masts beyond the stone cottages. Boats were ten a penny in the estuary, bringing jute or whale oil, but a Spanish boat was news indeed. The customers were full of it when they came in for their daily provisions. It was sheltering from the storm for a couple of days and, having been battered by ferocious winds coming up the east coast, it needed to have one of its sails repaired.

Janet gave her husband her full attention now.

"Well, I've bought the cargo of oranges," he said, obviously delighted with his news.

She gazed at him in horror. Her mind went immediately to the locked box in the bedroom cupboard in which she kept any profit from the shop and all the money they possessed.

"I've used our savings," he said sheepishly, as if reading her mind, "but, Janet, think how much I'll be able to sell them for! Spanish oranges in the middle of winter. People will go mad for them – the sunshine of Spain captured in those small orange fruits. They will be a real novelty and everyone will want to taste one. I tell you, my dear Janet, we shall make three times the profit. We shall be rich!" He put his hands round her small waist and danced her round the shop until she smiled.

"Away with ye now." She straightened her white mob cap. *Wretched man,* she thought affectionately, *he can always get round me.*

Janet was the sensible one who kept the books, writing down down the goods they bought from local merchants, what they sold, and the meagre profit they made in the shop. After they closed, she would work by candlelight, never satisfied until the numbers tallied each day. James was the talker who could charm the customers with his blether. As for their son, Young Jamie, well he was barely out of his teens and made little effort as he really didn't want to spend his days in the shop anyway.

"Why isn't the captain getting one of his men to sell them?" Janet asked.

"Well, he's leaving on the early evening tide. There will be a fair wind to take them to Edinburgh this night. He hasn't time to sell oranges, Janet." Her husband smiled. "What a bargain."

"So you said, James."

"Young Jamie is down at the quay even now organising the carts."

"Carts? How many did you buy?"

"Twenty crates."

"Twenty! Have you taken leave of your senses?"

All Janet could think of was that there would be no money to pay the miller or the sugar merchant next week.

When the cart rumbled over the flagstones, James went outside to help their son unload the crates of oranges and carry them through the shop to the storeroom at the back. It was crowded so they had to move sacks of flour and sugar before they could find a space and the crates were piled to the roof when they left the storeroom. James was full of enthusiasm for his purchase, planning to build a pyramid of oranges in the shop window before they opened next day.

That evening, he prised the lid off a wooden crate with a crowbar and took out three oranges and carried them to the kitchen, the only room behind the shop. After their mutton and barley broth, they sat full of anticipation as Janet brought three of her best plates and sharp knives. They peeled them carefully; this would be a rare treat for the family.

They were sour.

So bitter, Janet couldn't eat more than a mouthful. Her husband blustered and tried to eat half of his orange, his face growing red in the process.

"You fool, husband, you've been sold oranges that no one can eat."

"But the captain assured me they were the very best oranges," said James, helpless in the face of her fury.

"Oh you – you'd believe anything!"

Janet burst into tears and ran up the stairs to the bedroom. She opened the money box and found one remaining guinea.

Later, when she heard her husband coming up the stairs, then getting undressed and climbing into bed, she kept her head turned away, still too distressed to speak. He tentatively stretched out his hand to touch her shoulder.

"Janet, I'm sorry . . ."

"Don't you dare touch me," she shouted. "You've ruined us!"

He withdrew his hand. He didn't say any more. What was there to say? He tried to make himself as small as possible and clung to his side of the bed.

Janet couldn't sleep. Usually, she was so tired after a day on her feet in the shop, she slept through the whole night until the dawn came in. She tossed and turned before finally groping her way down the narrow wooden stairs to light the candle. The fire was banked up until morning so the room was warm and cosy. Even looking at it filled her with despair; this had been their home for twenty two years. Are we to lose it all because of that man's stupidity?

She gave the fire a savage poke and it broke into flames which lit up the room.

On the far side, she could see the jars of preserves on the dresser: plum, blackberry, raspberry and gooseberry, all of which she'd made last autumn. She allowed herself a moment's pride as she surveyed the jars in their ordered rows, graded by the colour of the fruit.

There's the answer! It was right there in front of her. Orange Jam! She would turn all that fruit into orange jam.

Next day, energised, she was up early stirring the porridge over the fire when the two men came down.

"Now you two will have to manage without me in the shop today," she said. "I'm making jam to sell from those oranges. The Lord knows we have to try and get some of the money back."

James went meekly from the room just pleased that her anger seemed to have abated during the night. He dragged a crate through to the kitchen for her.

By eight o'clock, she was hard at work, peeling, cutting, and boiling the oranges before adding sugar from a sack in the storeroom. In no time at all, she had six jars of jam set ready to sell. As she worked, she soon realised that she could not take on this mammoth task on her own. The oranges were beginning to dry and the skins to shrivel slightly; it was essential to get them cooked as quickly as possible. She would ask four of the women from the cottages nearby – all good jam-makers – to come to her kitchen to help. Janet would pay them as soon as the jam started to sell. The women would be glad to earn some extra money as their husbands had been laid off the whaling boats.

Soon all five of them were chopping, boiling and adding sugar, making jam as fast as they could physically manage it. The whole house and shop were filled with the tantalising, delicious smell of oranges cooking and as soon as it had set cold, Janet sent it through to be sold. As it was something new, customers asked if they could try a sample, before they bought the jam. James was happy to oblige, giving them a small spoonful each. He built his pyramid of oranges flanked by the new pots of jam.

As the day wore on, the women grew tired of cutting the white pith from the peel, so Janet instructed them to put it all in: "Just cut it into wee chunky strips, it'll all sell."

It was a surprising success. By the end of the day they had sold over seventy jars of the orange jam. James told his customers the strips of chunky peel were particularly good for the digestion, especially at breakfast time. The slightly bitter flavour was good for the stomach. He called it orange marmalade, a word that tumbled out of the back of his mind from his seafaring days.

"Marmalade is a peculiar name, James," a few said.

"Well, I'm told that when Mary Queen of Scots lived in France as a little girl she always asked for orange jam when she wasn't feeling well," he replied. "In France they would say, *Marie malade* (Mary's ill), so that's how we got the word marmalade." It was a more satisfying explanation than the Portuguese word *marmelos*, which had been used for centuries, he thought to himself.

"Orange marmalade sounds a wee bit tame, James," Janet said as she started placing another fifty jars on the shelf. "Can you think of another name?"

"How about Dundee Marmalade, my love?"

He placed his hands round her small waist and did a polka round the kitchen until she was out of breath and her smile was as broad as his.

Pigeon-holes

Sarah Palmer

My mother likes her pigeon-holes, and over the years they've proved handy storage. Every so often, during one of her extended visits up from the coast, she'll dust one off and there'll be a story about my aunt, your father's cousin, your grandmother.

But when she's wiping toast crumbs from the corner of her mouth and says your brother-in-law, I don't know who she means. Tapping at the *Daily Mail* splayed out on the kitchen table, she points at a blurred photograph, beckoning me over with her toast. I don't want to look at the *Daily Mail*, but sigh and peer over her shoulder at the CCTV still. I'd misunderstood. She hadn't said your brother-in-law, like she was starting a story. No, it was a question: your brother-in-law?

I pull the newspaper towards me. She's right, it is him, with his new name and new beard and apparent new-found ability to get out of bed before three o'clock in the afternoon. I would have turned the page without recognising him, since we stopped looking for him long ago. But somehow my mother clocked him, even though she only met him once, in a wedding line-up, when he was clean-shaven and happy to be called Stevo.

Later, when Mike's come back from work and rung the police, and his dad, and his other brother, and cried, my mother makes ham and cheese sandwiches for lunch and goes to have a nap.

Perhaps, if she hadn't been visiting at just the right time, she wouldn't have remembered him either, just glanced at the photograph like the rest of us and put him in some other pigeon-hole. Not had to sneak off to her bedroom with her mobile for a whispered conversation, my daughter's brother-in-law . . .

A Grandmother's Tears:
Pondering a Memory

Anne Dryden

"Do you ever cry, Gran?" I asked. She was always Gran, not Grandma or Granny and definitely not Nan. Her steel grey hair was neatly rolled and secured with u-shaped hairpins. I was once informed that it was actually long and straight, reaching right down her back. This bewildered me. Only young girls had long hair, didn't they? I tried to imagine how it would look as she smoothed it out using the broad silver-topped brush that I had seen on her dressing table. I also remember that her back was very bent. She wore a tweed suit, referred to as a tunic, thick flesh-coloured stockings and stout lace-up shoes (or tartan pompom-topped slippers) and used a stick to support her walking.

It was the late 1960s and I would have been six or seven years old, on a regular weekend visit to my grandparents' cottage. In my eagerness, I had tripped on the doorstep and came clattering down onto the flagstone floor, cutting my knee on the steel shoe scraper as I went. I let out a wail. It chorused with the piercing squeak of a brass tap being rotated and the metallic ping of the stream of water falling onto the enamel bowl in the butler sink below. Gran washed her hands with Wright's coal tar soap before cleaning my wound. I can still smell it now. I was pacified only once the trickle of blood had subsided, antiseptic had been applied, and a powdery yellow lemon bonbon was tucked away in my cheek.

My grandparents, Albert and Mabel, were older than all my friends' grandparents. They had been born in the last decade of Queen Victoria's reign and were married on Boxing Day in 1916, as the country mourned for the young men already lost in the Great War battles of Ypres, Gallipoli and the Somme. They lived all their lives in the village of Coleford in Somerset, whose main purpose, it seems, was to supply young able-bodied men to labour in the mines of the North Somerset coalfield. A certificate hung on the wall in their low-ceilinged kitchen, advising anyone who paused to read it that Albert had served for 52 years in the coal industry. Several blue scars on his arms hinted that most of those years were spent underground. My grandfather was never a soldier. He completed his national service obligation by supplying coal to keep the wheels of industry turning. I wish now that I had asked him more about his working life. All I remember is being told he filled a large jug every night with water boiled in a kettle on the range, and in the morning, before he departed for his shift underground, he drank the cooled water. Before the aforementioned tap had been plumbed in, water was pumped from a well just outside the back door. Probably it was sensible to boil this water and the habit had continued. Or perhaps the tap water was not trusted like the well water. Either way, to a child of six years, it seemed a mysterious thing for someone to do. It was the often-quoted opinion of the family that this daily ritual contributed to his longevity, for Albert went on to reach the grand age of 96, outliving his wife and two of his sons. He rode a motorbike until he was 88 and passed away in the same cottage he had lived in all his married life. His heart and lungs were donated for medical research as it was so surprising, given his years breathing in pit dust, that he had made such old bones. Mabel gave birth to their four children in the bedroom upstairs in that cottage, also. All boys. The first was born in early 1918, the last in 1924. I often wonder who assisted her. Later, she became one of the first women to benefit from the newly formed National Health Service. In 1948, she missed my parents' wedding to undergo surgery to repair a prolapsed womb, a condition she had suffered from for years, most likely brought about by poor midwifery care.

After a pause, Gran replied to my question. "I cried all my tears away when your uncle was sent to Burma in the war. I have no more tears left."

In recent years, as my own children have become young adults, I have pondered over this admission by my grandmother. Certainly, I wept like a baby after waving my son and daughter off to the perils of university life. Yet when Neville Chamberlain declared war on Germany in his radio broadcast of September 1939, my grandparents found themselves in the position of having four sons, three of military age and the youngest not far behind. Having already experienced the horrors of the Great War, Mabel's heart must surely have frozen that day, in anticipation of another global conflict.

It is not that she would have been unused to living with menfolk in ever present danger. She was a miner's wife after all.

The village had known its share of tragedy. My grandfather's mother married two brothers. The first was killed when a fall of rock crushed him as he worked hewing coal. That would have been around 1880. Eleven years previously, in 1869, an explosion in the local Mackintosh pit killed seven men. One was my grandfather's great uncle who left a wife and eight children. A report states that there was no fund for the relief of the sufferers and the colliery owners paid for the funerals of the men. Albert worked in the mines from the age of twelve and would have been an experienced collier when on 9 April 1908 a blast ripped through neighbouring Norton Hill Colliery, killing ten including a fourteen year old boy.

As things turned out, my uncle, a grocer's assistant, the eldest son, returned from Burma after the war unharmed. Son number three, as a farmhand, was in an exempted occupation and not compelled to take up arms. My father, son number two, registered as a conscientious objector. This fact has at various times in my life made me feel emotions from shame, to indifference, to pride. It was never much spoken about, although I do recall my father telling me he had to attend a court hearing in Bristol. He became a Methodist lay preacher, and at the time would have been studying for this. His defence was that his God was the same God as the German soldiers': how could he pray to Him for victory in battle?

Knowing now how my grandmother felt and the conversations that must have been had at the time around the scrubbed-topped kitchen table in the cottage in Somerset, I can't help wondering if there was more to my father's determination not to go to war. Perhaps he just couldn't bear to add to his mother's tears.

It is, however, the fate of the youngest son, Roy, that makes my grandmother's comment about her lack of tears so poignant. He was too young to serve at the outbreak of war, and I have no record of any military service that he may have done. Later, he followed his elder brother into the grocery business. By a cruel twist of fate, my Uncle Roy died of a medical condition in 1949 at the age of 24. My father never spoke of him and I don't recall my grandparents ever speaking of him. What I know comes from my mother. She said he was a very gentle man and the day he died was the only time she saw my father cry. So why was my grandmother's response not, "I cried all my tears after your uncle died."? Only a mother experiencing this loss can know. How deeply must my grandmother have buried those tears for her youngest boy.

How Will It End

Terence Brand

The howling wind plucked at my cliff-top home. Rain rattled against the window bay surrounding my desk. Shaken out of a fit of melancholy – lately, a not infrequent frame of mind – I peered through the quivering glass. An even stronger gust struck the darkening headland. Surf raced below. The incoming tide dashed suds of spray high above the cliff edge. Black clouds encroached on the setting sun, ushering premature night over the mounting seas.

Closer to the window, a solitary tree bent before the onslaught. Its branches flailed the path that led up from the nearby village.

Lights flashing in the glass caused me to look down into the valley. Headlamps floodlit the village street before dimming in the pub car park. I shook my head. What sort of people left their homes in such weather? And it could only get worse. It would be a wild night.

"So what?" I muttered. "Get back to work. You promised yourself you'd have the final chapter written by morning."

I dropped my eyes to the screen before me. Fluorescent words hung in the dusk; punched into the word processor some minutes before the sudden squall had snatched me from my bitter reverie. The screen glowed redly as a smouldering log collapsed in the fireplace behind me. Distracted, I looked around the room. Amid the shower of sparks, a last lick of flame danced chimney-ward, throwing flickering shadows from the meagre bits of furniture occupying the small room: the tall bookcase, untidy shelves proof of regular consultation; the lumpy, high-backed chair squatting in front of the fire; and, nudging the chair's arm, the low table scattered with leftovers from a lonely meal.

I stretched for Roget. Opening the fat book under the pool of light from an angle-poise lamp, I riffled the pages. Off-spring was not right. Progeny? Descendant? Get? Issue? Seed?

I slammed the book shut; I was only picking at an itching wound. I missed my daughter. I hadn't seen or heard tell of her since she had swept out of the cottage on a dark and stormy night much like this, ten years ago. Ten years to the very day. The sentences flowing across the screen had spewed from my subconscious, generated by the sultry atmosphere and a mind preoccupied with the sad anniversary.

The argument that day had been long and passionate. I had mustered all the old prejudices, all the reasons a father dredges up to prove a man was not good enough for his daughter, whether I believed them or not.

"He's so young. You're both so young. And what are his prospects, working in that garage? Do you really want to marry a grease-monkey?"

"Oh, father, that's not fair. Barry has passed all his City and Guilds. He's a valued mechanic. He'll be getting a rise very soon."

"That's all very well, but where are you going to live? In his poky little hole above the bookie?"

Jennie's eyes flashed. "Why not? Mummy told me that you two had to live with her parents for the first two years. At least Barry's able to rent a decent flat."

She was right. But I merely shrugged. "The world was different then."

I was well aware how lame my objections were. In truth, I couldn't bear to part with my little girl. She had been my constant companion; her mother had died when she was very young. I hadn't wanted the days of sunshine and laughter to end. To me, my child had never grown up.

And so, with no thought as to how hurtful my resistance was, I searched for more and more reasons in my desperate attempts to keep her near me. Until the inevitable outcome. Eugenie, exasperated beyond endurance, stormed off to pack.

Through the empty years which followed my daughter's tearful departure I came to realise how foolish I had been. If I had given my blessing I could have continued to play a part in her life.

But it was too late. Eugenie had gone. I had lost my little Jennie.

Life became a drudge; my writing suffered. I aged and was always tired. Not until I confronted myself with the truth did I begin to come to terms with my loss. I poured my anguish into the novel which now fills the memory of my computer. I sensed I was writing with a poignancy that could put me back on the bestseller list after a decade's absence.

But how to end?

I had been working on the last chapter for months. The writing was emotive, even powerful, but the emotion was despair, the power cataclysmic. Try as I might, I could not draw my characters into a fulfilling denouement.

Having consumed the log, the fire dulled. Outside, the wind advanced to gale force. My gaze was lured back to the elemental scene. The sun had given up the unequal battle, vanquished by the hurrying cumulus. A sheet of lightning lit the rocky track and silhouetted the beleaguered tree. Rain began to fall in earnest.

When the world beyond the window vanished – doused by the dark aftermath of the static discharge – the glass mirrored a pair of eyes; hooded eyes in the face of a man old before his time. A drawn, lost face.

My face.

A deep bellow of thunder depressed my eardrums. It seemed to echo the question going through my mind.

What am I doing here?

I shook my head. I had no answer.

The buffeting wind groaned under the rafters and whistled in the branches of the genuflecting tree. The telephone on my desk burbled for attention only to be stifled mid-ring.

Simultaneously, my desk lamp and the computer screen winked out.

Patiently, I waited for my sight to adjust to the gloom. It was not unusual to lose power and communication during a gale. The cottage was served by vulnerable overhead cables. I had installed a petrol-driven generator for use when the lines were severed. I reached down to the drawer in which I kept matches and candles.

As I scrabbled for the candles something slapped against the windowpane. Jerking upright, candle in hand, I stared into the dark night, apprehensively this time: debris, hurled into the air by a swirling wind, could break a window.

Seeing no evidence of damage, I found a match, scratched it and applied the burning end to a candle.

Again an object smacked the glass, this time remaining pressed to the surface. I raised my fragile light. The flame's glow picked out a hand. A callused, deathly white, skeletal hand. It appeared to be cut off at the wrist.

I stared at the disembodied member. Melting tallow scalded me unnoticed as I watched the gaunt fingers close over the horny palm to make a fist.

One gnarled digit extended, and then crooked to beckon.

Despair hit me. In my fevered imagination the Angel of Death was calling. My story was to end here. My characters were to be abandoned in turmoil. The final chapter would be left unresolved.

Worse – much worse – I should never know if my Jennie had found the happiness she deserved.

A fit of pique took hold of me. Intent on arguing my case with the Grim Reaper, I leaned forward and unlatched a side window.

The eerie hand uncurled, gripped the frame and pulled it aside. Black oilskin flapped, revealing a brawny arm.

Jem Tresilian's weather-beaten features rose above the sill. Needles of rain lashed his streaming sou'wester. "Come on, John," he shouted over the tumult, "get your wellies – you'll have to walk down to the village, the track's flooded."

"Why should I want to go to the village?" I cried, astonishment overwhelming my relief.

"Because the car can't get up the hill."

"Whose car?"

"Didn't she get through?" Old Jem grinned. "Jennie's here," he yelled. "She and her husband and their little ones are in the pub. We're celebrating. But it's you they came to visit!"

Heart jumping, I threw on wet-weather clothing. Splashing through puddles in Jem's wake, I grunted with exasperation: the power failure had wiped the final chapter from the computer.

I cleared a small lake with an exuberant leap. It didn't matter; I'd always known I would have to rewrite the chapter. And now I knew how it ended!

Vanish

Liz Tait

I feel the heat of panic before I see her.

Running like she'd spent her life avoiding it, in sandals made for sauntering, not sprinting.

"Two boys – my grandchildren – blonde – have you seen them? Five and three?"

Oh God. Sheer terror, up close, her hand grips my arm.

"No, not that I . . ."

"Told them not to move! I'm checking the toilets!"

She was off, clutching her chest, before her sandals were ready, losing one briefly through a crack in the boardwalk. Her life changing ominously by the second.

"I'll look out for them!"

My planned tea and cake in the café now felt somewhat frivolous.

I see her clutch other strangers, dragging them into the unfolding dark of her day. Strewn like fallen skittles in her wake.

I shade my eyes to look out over the beach, heavily dotted with stripy towels, strewn paddle-boards and laughing children.

I am aware of a feeling. It is relief.

Because this was me, this thing was exactly me, yesterday. We were here at about this time. My granddaughter and I.

Her ice cream dripped everywhere and I found myself wet-wipe-less. That was the extent of my "nightmare". Her yellow sunflower dress now soaks in Vanish stain remover at home. Hopefully the evidence will be gone and my daughter will never know . . .

Yesterday was windy and cold, not really ice cream weather but Jess, my granddaughter, grumpily refused the apple rice-cake offered. Her mother reminded me later that she didn't like the apple-flavoured rice cakes.

"You knew that, Mum?!"

Today the sun shines in spite.

There's something a little eerie about the pier. Its façade marinated with decades of candy floss and sweat. Never-funny clowns leer from the twists of the Helter-Skelter tower.

The sea swaggers below, hungry for a sacrificial offering.

Please, not today.

I'm thankful for my walk-on part. Spectator. I don't thank God.

Another Nana with ill-fitting sandals and two missing grandchildren has the starring role.

I'm grateful for someone else's pain. Truth be told.

Time to move. I continue my walk to the café. There's nothing else I can do, is there?

I pass young, blonde boys everywhere, clutching parents' hands. Skipping and hopping and belonging. They all look like they belong. They all look aged five and three. Not lost.

Suddenly, two boys and a woman run past me. Careless Nana pushes me out of the way, her screams of delight piercing, arms open in ecstatic relief. The crowd breaks into delighted applause at the reunion. I do the same.

"Oh my God, that stupid wasp, I'm so sorry darling . . . I turned round . . . damn thing wouldn't leave me alone!"

Nana's daughter smiles kindly at her.

"It's okay mum – they found me in the cafe . . ."

"But I told them to stay in the arcade!"

"We couldn't find you, Nanny!" The younger boy sobs.

Mother and daughter are hugging. They're all hugging.

"Can we have ice cream now?!"

It is over.

I am aware of a feeling. It is envy.

Saturday Child

Paul Doran

One Saturday a man came to take me out. My mam says, "It's OK, he's your dad," and the man says, "Yes, I'm your dad."

But I didn't know who this man was. I didn't know I had a dad, and I thought it might be good if I did, 'cos I was the only one at school who didn't have a dad. When I asked my mam why he didn't live with us, she just said not all mams and dads lived together, but I didn't understand.

That day, and on other Saturdays, the man called Dad took me out and he bought me me things: sweets and books, anything I wanted.

We'd go to the cinema and sometimes the park for me to play on the swings. Sometimes we'd go on the bus or the train, sometimes quite far, to a place called Brighton. I liked it there, better than Worthing.

He liked football so we went to see some and he thought I should like it too. I didn't, but I didn't tell him.

Once, when we were in McDonald's, he was on his mobile phone a long time and when I tried tell him I needed to go to the toilet he got cross and he told me to be quiet and to do my colouring or read my book. I wet my pants and I cried 'cos I didn't know what I'd done wrong.

One day when we went to the park we met a woman he seemed to know.

She was a nice woman and he seemed to like her more than me.

He told me not to tell my mam but I did and she got cross and cried. I put my arm around her and asked her what was wrong. She just said, "Son you're too young to understand, but there's nothing for you to worry about."

So I didn't worry, but the man called dad stopped coming to take me out.

24

Maud

Roger Shadbolt

Homeleigh Nursing Home, as bright as the fresh flowers arranged around the day room, not a wilting bloom in sight, bearing witness to the sign hanging above the entrance: "Homeleigh – Your Home From Home".

Matron approaching, her smile almost as broad as her waistline. "There's someone to see you, Maud."

Maud, propped up in her daybed, surrounded by cushions, a few strands of grey hair escaping from under the magenta scarf tied around her head.

"I don't need to see anyone, I see enough of you lot already."

"Now then Maud, I want you to be polite this time if you can."

"As long as it's not that tosser who was walking round last week with a clipboard, asking lots of stupid questions."

"He was only doing his job."

"He didn't look as if he'd ever done a proper job in his life."

"It was to do with your welfare, Maud. He was from Health & Safety, making sure you were being properly looked after."

"So where was he hiding when they tried to give all of us the Covid? Kill us all off so they wouldn't have to keep paying our pensions? Someone should have swung for that."

"This person is a nice young lady reporter from the local newspaper."

"What's she reporting me for? I haven't done anything, I can't, lying here in this bed all day with you lot fussing around."

"She wants to interview you for an article and I'd like you to be on your best behaviour."

"I hope she's not some young tart with a short skirt and high heels, it would likely give George over there a heart attack. Anyway, I'm not giving her my life story, I haven't finished with it yet."

A neatly dressed young woman approaching, her pretty face framed by soft blonde curls of hair. "Good morning, Maud. I'm so pleased to meet you. My name's Julia and I'm interviewing our more experienced citizens for a follow-up piece to the one I wrote for the Queen's Jubilee."

"The Queen? Now there was a real lady, God rest her soul. I wouldn't have wanted her job; had to smile when she met all those foreigners, crooks most of them. Charlie's got the job now,. He's had his ups and downs, terrible dancer, always out of time with the music. Are you going to use one of those lapbob things to record me?"

"No, I use an iPad these days, Maud. You ought to get one."

"The only pads I use these days, dear, are the ones they give me in case I can't get to the loo in time. Arthritis, you see. Used to be a runner for our school you know; war put a stop to that. Trouble with those lapbob things is nobody writes letters anymore. I had a cupboard full of letters I'd kept, love letters mostly, but I had to throw them away when I came here. Only got one small drawer, full of pills."

"I overheard you mention Covid, Maud. Do you mind me asking if you caught the virus?"

"No, I didn't. These days, the germs take one look at me and bugger off. Bill in the next bed wasn't so lucky, he caught it on his 90th. They wheeled him up to the window wearing a mask and all his family stood outside in the rain jumping up and down shouting 'Happy Birthday'. Complete waste of time – he was stone deaf. Poor sod died two days later."

Julia, glancing round the room. "It must have been such a terrible time for everyone."

"It was, dear. The staff in here were all running about like headless chickens scared stiff they were going to take the Covid home with them all, wearing those silly little masks, completely hopeless. We had proper masks in the war, great black things made of rubber that covered the whole of your face and smelt horrible. We used to frighten people with them."

"You must have been a teenager during the war, Maud. Can I ask you about your memories of that time, if it's not too painful?"

"You can ask what you like, dear. My father was a docker and we lived in the East End during the Blitz, until I was evacuated. I've seen arms and legs sticking out of the rubble with nobody attached to them. Wales was a lot safer but it rained most of the time and we didn't get to play all the games we'd invented down in the tube stations. The other thing I remember were the bloomin' Yanks, they were everywhere. Their hands were everywhere too; I had one of them want to take me back to his ranch in Texas. I was pretty in those days."

"I'm sure you were, Maud. Weren't you tempted to go?"

"Not bloomin' likely, the whole place was covered with cows and whorehouse. That wasn't for me."

"Did you have a sweetheart during the war, then?"

"Not me; our real sweetheart was Vera, used to listen to her all the time on the radio. What a voice she had, sang like a bird she did, mezzo-soprano you know. Oh, and Winnie."

"Winnie?"

"Winston of course, what a man. Told everybody exactly what he thought of them. He and Vera won the war for us. I used to sing a bit in those days, in the church choir. Not as good as her, of course."

"You were a churchgoer then?"

"No I wasn't. God lets too many bad things happen. I went so I could sneak off with the boy who sang the tenor solos and smoke cigarettes behind the vestry." Maud, lying back with the hint of a chuckle.

"Was he your boyfriend then Maud?"

"No. but I wish he had been. My first real boyfriend got me pregnant, just about the only thing he was good for. We got married of course – you had to in those days. He never did a stroke of work so I got rid of him as soon as I could, thank goodness. It took me a while to find my second husband. Men were in short supply after the war. He was older than me and wasn't exactly Errol Flynn, but he was a good man and looked after me. He passed away a long while back."

Julia, looking down at her notes. "That reminds me. I only know you as Maud. I don't have your surname."

Maud, pointing her finger. "It's Shadwell. Make sure you get the 'D', in the middle. I used to have trouble with some of my pupils turning it into a 'G'."

"You were a teacher, Maud?"

"Head teacher. East Ham primary."

"Oh, well done you. Did you enjoy teaching?"

"The kids were alright, the local authority were rubbish. I wouldn't do that job now; it's all about filling in forms."

"So tell me about your own children, Maud. Do they keep in touch? How many did you have?"

Maud looking down at her blankets for a moment. "Can you pass me a tissue from that box dear, my eyes get a bit smeary sometimes. They keep the heating up so high in here. Thank you. I had a boy and a girl. They're both gone now."

"I'm so sorry to hear that, Maud."

"Do you have any children, Julia?"

Julia, smiling, eyes lighting up. "Not yet, but we're hoping to start a family soon."

"If you do, try and arrange to die before they do. It's better that way round."

"I'll try and remember that, Maud."

Matron returning. "Julia had better go now, Maud, lunch is being brought round."

"You see how they order you about in here, Julia? Mind you, the food's not bad, apart from the Italian Ragout."

"Goodbye, Maud. It's been a real pleasure talking to you."

"Goodbye dear, and remember to spell my name right. I don't want any trouble from this lot in here."

"I'll remember, Maud."

Hair Today, Gone Tomorrow

Liz Tait

She's seen me. She's smiling. It costs nothing.

"Hi Jo, long time no see! Have you just had your hair done in there, naughty girl?!"

Her Pashmina's whipping me in the wind. I had no idea they were still a thing. I'm babbling, she's circling.

"Er, yes, just, I just . . . spur of the moment, you know how it is."

Any minute now she's going to lift my chin up like a Crufts judge.

"You've had the colour done as well, haven't you? Bloody lucky to get an appointment there on the 'spur of the moment'. For all that!"

I could leg it but she's all over my exit routes.

"You know I'd have given you a call first, obviously, because you – I mean, you've always been my, you always do my hair, don't you, but you don't work Wednesdays, so . . ."

My pants are well and truly on fire. Her indignation warms the back of my neck.

"I do! I've always worked Wednesdays. Hey, it doesn't matter, does it? You can get your hair done where you like, can't you? Don't be silly."

She's going to say it.

"It's a free country!"

It's not, though. Not when it comes to hair. It's very far from free. It's a tangled, whole-months'-salary-gone-in-a-hair-toss minefield. One snip by a rival blade and you'll never get a complimentary fringe trim anywhere in this town again.

Now she's touching my freshly-razored neck. I wonder if she knows.

She snatches my Keira Knightley picture out of my hand.

"Keira Knightley? Oh my God, is this a break-up cut?"

Don't snatch.

"'New hair, new me' sort of thing?"

Break-down cut, if you must know.

She doesn't know.

"You wanted to look like this?!"

I wanted Keira back.

"Does make me laugh when my clients bring photos in. I always say 'You know I'm just a hair stylist, not a plastic surgeon, don't you? Can't work miracles!'"

It's starting to rain on my new hair. I wish for the millionth time I was the umbrella-carrying type.

"Not long now then?"

Oh God, did I just say that? Must have done, my finger's pointing at the bump in her protective hands.

"The nineteenth. Two weeks. CANNOT WAIT! Gotta go, busting for the loo, as usual. Lovely to see you!"

She's rounding up the pashmina. I've got away with it.

"Hey, wait, yours must be . . . how is . . . you had a girl, right?"

Shit.

"Is she in nursery already? Bloody lucky to get her in somewhere! Which one's she at?"

Almost.

"She's not anywhere. She died. One hour 36 minutes after she was born."

Hands abandon brewing belly to fly stricken to her gaping mouth.

Saying it feels a tiny bit easier every time. The dance of confused, embarrassed horror – not easier. Never easier.

Rain hammers the pavement between us.

I watch her waddle away, then she kind of does this last-minute swerve into Greggs. Pretty sure they don't have toilets in there.

My hair feels flat and sticky. I should go home.

I jump, Norman Wisdom style, to a tap on the back. I turn and Melanie's showing me a piece of heart-shaped shortbread with a bloodshed-red jammy heart in a Greggs bag.

She pulls me into a wet hug then she's gone, trusty pashmina trailing behind.

And I'm eating it, now, in the rain. I'm hungry. So damn hungry.

Five currant buns in a Baker's Shop,

Fat and round with a cherry on the top.

Forgot how much I love shortbread.

Along came a boy with a penny one day

Bought a currant bun and took it away!

Stupid song rattles around my derelict head. I've asked nicely for it to stop. Please, for pity's sake, stop now.

Forgot how much I love Ed, who has silently, under the cover of darkness, undone our house of baby things.

I want to go home.

The Problem
Was Slowly Draining Away

John Rudkin

The dominant colour outside of the bus window is a muddy, fawnish grey. The splattered dirt throws back the reflected interior light and highlights me in all my ageing glory and that is even greyer and growing more-so by the day. A tune is playing in the back of my mind and I have to concentrate to work out what it is. Then it comes to me and makes me smile, "A Whiter Shade of Pale" recorded by Procol Harum in the summer of 1967, when, as a father for the first time, life was much rosier and so was my complexion.

The bus is now entering the edge of the city and some of my gloomy mood is lifting. A few years ago this section of town had almost as many closed retail outlets as those that were open. Later, some of them became charity shops, but now things appear to be looking up a little and brightly lit new premises are taking their places. Admittedly, most of these are mobile phone stores, nail bars and the latest fad, the "vape" emporiums that provide the alternative for the steam-suckers that seem to be replacing the smokers. To be fair to the "vapes" though, they aren't peddling suicide, unlike the tobacco sellers.

I turn my attention to the upper storeys of the shops, which are mostly Edwardian or Victorian and have plaques that say "Forest View" or "Park Terrace", followed by the date they were built. 1898 or 1901 seem to be the most common. There must have been massive building programmes in these periods, much the same as that which is happening today. The forest has been cut down long ago and the parkland has been swallowed up by the ever-encroaching city buildings.

Now the bus is nearly in the city centre and I ring the bell. I am going to transfer to the "Open Topped Tour Bus". Hopping off, alighting, as it used to say on the notices, although I've never heard anyone actually say "alighting". I walk the fifty of so yards to the tour bus stop and join the queue. There's only five other

31

people waiting and the bus arrives almost immediately.

The weather looks cloudy and it will probably rain, so no one except me climbs the stairs to the upper deck. I sit in one of the front seats and feel a little nervous. Beth and I used to travel all over the country together, her giving talks and teaching workshops, me acting as a "roadie" and then manning the sales table. Beth has passed away now though, so I feel that if I visit any town we had visited together it would upset me and if it was a town we hadn't been to then I'd feel equally upset that we'd never got around to going there together. Sounds silly, I know, but after hardly ever being out of each other's sight for thirty years it sort of makes sense to me. Our grown up children always warned us that we were living in each other's pockets.

I came up with this plan whereby I would force myself to tour a city, not too far away, and see what happened. So, here I am and the bus is now pulling away.

Strangely, I am getting good memories as the journey progresses, not like I expected it would be at all but then, almost as the trip ends, I spot this upstairs tea room and I can see people, mostly couples, chatting and smiling as they enjoy their tea and cakes. It reminds me of the Willow Tearooms in Glasgow. There's a lump in my throat. I'm beginning to feel very sad and I reach for my handkerchief. Now, though, my left shoulder begins to feel warm and I know I'm not alone. I turn and look but I can't see her. Nevertheless I recognise the feel.

I have set out to lay ghosts. Thank goodness I've failed.

Lost At Sea

Bill Garrod

The middle of the night and I was sailing on my own, north through the Inner Hebrides towards that lovely old village so loved in the children's TV series, Tobermory on the Isle of Mull. It was a filthy night. The wind was blowing close to gale force with big waves and intermittent rain showers which felt like pieces of ice hitting my face. However, all was well with the boat. Sails reefed down and the autohelm was holding her nicely on the pre-programmed course. Time for a mug of tea, I thought. Filled the kettle and lit the gas, which promptly failed.

"Bugger, need to change the bottle," I said to myself.

I opened the cockpit locker to gain access to the special gas bottle holder when the boat was struck by a very big wave. I was thrown across and almost overboard. Thank God for safety harnesses. The cockpit half filled with water and all the electrics failed. No lights or instruments. I grabbed the steering tiller to prevent a capsize. I got the boat settled and thought I was lost. The only instrument still working was the magnetic steering compass which was luminous and meant I could follow a course. But what course? The course to steer was now lost in the defunct autohelm and I couldn't call for help. No electrics, no radio.

Suddenly, a voice said, "Mister McAndrew, steer two-four-five degrees until you see a flashing green light."

"Who are you?" I shouted.

"I am the spirit of all mariners lost at sea," the voice replied. "Mister McAndrew, you are needed by your family. You must not be lost."

I brought the boat onto the course he said and it reminded me of the course I had originally set into the autohelm. He was right and after maybe twenty minutes through the gloom I saw a flashing green light.

"Now, Mister McAndrew," came the voice again. "Go round the buoy and head north on a course of three-four-five until you see the light from the lighthouse on the end of the Isle of Mull. Head towards the light and when daylight comes you will see the island."

I did as instructed and shouted, "Thank you and please tell me more about yourself!" My shout was in vain. He did not reply.

The weather began to ease and the sailing became enjoyable and told me there was a reason why I loved it so much. True to the spirit's word, as daylight came so did the outline of the island. I followed the land round the end of the island and mid-morning entered that lovely harbour with the many coloured houses reflected in the water.

Now to do something I had not done in years: sail onto a mooring buoy. No power so no engine. I succeeded at the third attempt. I was really chuffed. I stowed the sails and tidied the boat.

Right, time for that delayed mug of tea. I again opened the cockpit locker and the first thing I saw was that the main isolating switch from the batteries was off. I switched it on and all the electrics came to life. God, when I fell I must have accidentally hit that switch. I switched off all the now-unneeded instruments, changed the gas and made my long awaited mug of tea.

With my tea, I sat down to write the log entry for the voyage. Poised with my pen and looking at the page I wondered if anyone reading the log in the future would believe I had a visit from the spirit of all mariners lost at sea.

Rotherford Hall:
Christmas 1851

Norman Allcorn

In 1851, the 250 acres of Rotherfield Hall had been farmed by the Allcorn Family for over 100 years. So long that many people thought that they owned it. However, it was rented, with the family preferring to put their capital into stock and crops. That left them open to the whims of the landlord, and now he wanted to farm it himself. They had been given notice to quit by September 1852.

The tenant, 75 year old Elizabeth Allcorn, was determined that, as this was their last Christmas, it would be a good one. She was running the farm with the last of her ten children, her son Fred. Fred was a bachelor at 34 who showed no signs of getting married, being more interested in the farm and his prize Sussex cattle. This worried Elizabeth and she could see no suitable bride. Then she thought of Ann Moon, a widow from Treblers, the farm next door. Ann was 39 and had four children, but still young enough to have some more. But how to get them together? Of course, a big Christmas party. It would only be right to invite her and her family along with all the other friends and relations. Plenty of food and drink and the Mayfield Mummers for entertainment.

The party was over, the food and drink consumed. The mummers had performed. St George had killed the Turkish Knight and the Spanish Doctor had brought him back to life.

It was then time for Ann to get the children home to bed. She went into the kitchen to light her lantern. Elizabeth said that Fred will see them home. He had no choice but to agree: "Just let me get my boots on and light my lantern."

They went out of the back door and pass the cattle sheds. Several pairs of yellow eyes picked out by the lights. The youngest child, Liz, speaks up.

"Mr Allcorn is it true that the oxen pray to baby Jesus at

35

midnight on Christmas eve?"

He thought quickly. "Well, I am normally in bed by then, unless I go to midnight mass, but one thing I do know is that they are always practising." He called out to the bullocks and kicked the wooden feed trough. One by one the dark red Sussex steers rose from their elbows to their feet. (Horses and donkeys get up with their front legs straight but sheep and cows get up on their elbows first. In this position they look as if they are praying.)

"Oh, look at at that," cried out the younger girls.

"But that is what they always –" said their elder brother, but Ann put a hand on his arm and stopped him.

"Yes, they are always practising," she said. "Here, George, take my lantern for the girls. I can see by Mr Allcorn's." Then she stumbled, and clutched at his sleeve.

"Here, you had better take my arm," said Fred, which was what she wanted anyway.

On the way, they they talked about all things farming, which was unusual for Fred as he was shy with women, despite having sisters. When they reached Treblers, Ann asked if he would like to come in for a mince pie and a hot toddy. Fred said that he had an early start so had better not. He immediately regretted this, but too late. He now had to say goodbye. Did he shake hands or what?

Ann solved this for him. She leant forward and gave him a quick peck on the cheek. "Thanks for a lovely party."

Then she was gone.

Fred's heart was beating a lot faster. How could a little kiss do that? Something had happened but he could not figure out what. Anyway, he had agreed to look at her barley in the new year.

Fred married Ann at St Anne's Church, Lewes, on 1 September 1852. Why not at St Denys, Rotherfield, their parish church? Perhaps because a little Fred, my great grandfather, came along early in the new year. He was christened on 18 January and this time it was at St Denys. They should have known better at their age, surely!

The Interview

Roger Shadbolt

Steve had been very clear about the CV problem: "Don't worry about it old chap, nobody bothers to read them anymore. They're mostly online anyway and simply get deleted along with everything else."

"This one's a 16-page folder."

"Really? Doesn't make any difference, I haven't come across a man yet who reads beyond the cover sheet of any document. Forget it and find some common ground to talk about, like schooldays or rugby."

"The senior partner who's interviewing me is a woman, I doubt if she plays rugby."

Steve's face lit up. "Even better, Richard, it'll be a breeze for a good-looking chap like you. Just treat it like a first date, Be attentive but don't stare, smile a lot but don't grin, and above all don't try and tell any jokes. I've been interviewed by three women in my time; I finished up dating two of them. The third swung the other way so I got the job but that was all."

Richard wasn't entirely convinced. He couldn't really remember his first date but something told him it had been a bit of a disaster. Steve had never been renowned for his finesse or his modesty, but on the other hand his rise up the corporate ladder had been nothing less than meteoric, so he was always worth listening to.

He was still thinking "First date" as he followed her down a short corridor. Nice figure, smartly dressed and a slight hint of perfume. Perhaps Steve had a point.

She opened a door and showed him into a large, comfortably furnished lounge. "Please make yourself at home. As you will appreciate, Richard, many of our older" – she paused for emphasis – "and wealthier clients prefer to conduct their business in the comfort of their own homes, so we often use this room for interviews as it creates a similar environment and is more realistic."

That made sense, he thought, and settled himself into a large leather armchair. She sat down opposite him on a two-seater settee, her tight black skirt riding up above her knees. Nice legs too, he thought, must try not to stare. He shifted his gaze to the large circular clock that hung on the wall above her head. A long second hand moved round the numerals with a tick that was only just discernible. He moved his eyes down again and saw with some unease that she was fingering his CV, which lay open beside her.

"Now then, a few personal details to start with, You've been married for ten years, but no children yet." He nodded. "Never mind, many people these days are choosing to build their families later in life."

Where did that one come from? He couldn't see that it had any relevance to his job application. Perhaps she was trying to unsettle him, best not to respond.

She turned to the next page of his CV. "You've applied for the job of Senior Stockbroker, a position you already hold with your current firm." She paused. "And indeed you seem to have held for a number of years."

He was ready for that one, and had gambled that she probably wouldn't know his position was in fact a junior one, and he certainly wasn't going to mention the number of failed interviews he'd attended. "Well, I believe that loyalty is a very important part of our business."

"That's very commendable. In my job, I interview a large number of aspiring young men who seem to believe that changing their employer every year is an effective way of enhancing their career prospects."

She crossed one leg over the other and her skirt rode a little further up her thigh. He felt a slight movement around the area of his groin. Oh no, not now please! He locked one leg tight against the other hoping she wouldn't notice.

She turned her attention to his CV again. "Given the importance of the role that you currently undertake, the salary you are receiving seems, let me say, rather modest."

He'd already inflated it as much as he dared, as well as prepared an additional response. "That's true, but we are entitled to receive a substantial performance-related bonus every year." He gave her a broad smile, hoping it wasn't in danger of turning into a grin.

She smiled back at him. "So I assume you would have received a significant sum last year. Do you mind me asking how you spent some of it? Only, it's the kind of question we like to ask our clients in order to get an idea of their lifestyle and priorities."

He thought quickly. "Well, just the usual things really, a new Lexus, nothing too fancy." He shot a quick glance at the window hoping she couldn't see his old Toyota parked outside from where she was sitting. "And of course, a nice holiday in the sun."

"Where did you go?"

"Oh, well, Spain of course, the Costa Brava, we find it very relaxing there."

She raised her eyebrows. "Ah, yes, and a good deal cheaper than the Bahamas."

He decided to ignore that one, although the implication was obvious and he had the nasty feeling he might be starting to sweat a bit. He passed his hand across his forehead and was relieved to find his palm came back dry.

She'd noticed, however. "Are you finding it a bit warm in here? I think somebody has failed to adjust the heating."

Whoever somebody was, Richard suspected they might be receiving a bit of a rocket. She began removing her jacket, revealing a crisp white blouse. One size too small, he mused. The buttons seemed to be straining to retain her rather ample chest. The movement in his groin increased, and he wished there was a desk or table between them. He tried crossing one leg over the other, which didn't do much to help.

She didn't appear to see anything amiss. "Of course, these days we deal in international markets and one has to keep abreast of the different ways they move and the timescales in which they operate."

He uncrossed his legs and rubbed the back of his neck wondering where this was going. "Of course," he replied.

"So you will be familiar with the opening times of the different markets overseas. When, for example, does the Japanese stock market in Tokyo open for business?"

He was floored. Seeking inspiration, he looked towards the clock above her head but it simply stared back at him without giving anything away. The second hand seemed to have come to a halt as if waiting for his reply before moving on. He thought of New Year's Eve. Sydney was always first to set off their firework display, way ahead of the UK, and it was a similar part of the world. "Seven hours before us," he guessed. Her expression gave no indication as to whether he had been right or not so he carried on rapidly. "Of course, many of our clients are more comfortable investing closer to home in companies whose names they recognise, like Rolls-Royce and Shell. As a company, our watchword tends to be 'safety first'."

She leaned forward rather too enthusiastically. The top two buttons on her blouse gave up the unequal struggle and parted company revealing a significant amount of cleavage. "So you managed to avoid the worst effects of the 2008 stock market crash?"

The problem around his groin intensified and he struggled to maintain his composure. "Well, yes, we made extensive use of hedge funds to mitigate the impact on our client's portfolios." It was a complete lie; as a junior employee at the time, he had lost some of his own money that he could ill afford and some of his clients had lost a packet, costing him any chance of promotion. He didn't really know what hedge funds were but had a vague idea that they were a way of avoiding financial disasters.

To his great relief, she closed his CV with a flourish and sat back on the sofa. "Thank you for being so open with your answers. I think it's time that I told you a bit more about our firm and the type of benefits you can expect to receive."

Mirroring her, he relaxed back into his armchair. He couldn't help being mesmerised by the way in which the rest of her body moved as she waved her hands about in order to emphasise various aspects of the employment contract, most of which were vastly superior to his existing one.

Eventually, she stood up, smoothing down her skirt. "Thank you for coming to see us Richard. I hope this will turn out to be the start of a very profitable relationship."

Standing up, he took a step towards her and kissed her full on the mouth. "What say I crack open a bottle of St Emilion and we go to bed?"

"Sounds like a plan."

He walked into the kitchen and selected a bottle from the wine rack.

She'd caught him out about the Japanese stock exchange, and the crack about cheap Spanish holidays had been a bit below the belt, but overall he felt it had gone pretty well. He was lucky to have a wife who was head of an HR department and knew the right sort of questions to ask, in order for him to practise his interview technique.

He decided he wouldn't dwell too much on the thought of her interviewing a lot of aspiring young men.

The Reunion

Cherrie Taylor

"Not a good look!"

I try to ignore your whisper. But, well yes, not a good look. Deirdre never did know what suited her, but a lime green shorty with matching leggings!

Her smile is the same – always so open, so happy, so forgiving.

We smile back and go to find old girls we have something in common with.

The School Reunion is a seven-year event. I'd missed the one in 2013 – well, avoided it. The one in 2006 was a riot and I needed an extra seven years to recover.

"I hope you're not going to lose it this time," you say.

"I'm cool," I say. "The tablets are helping."

I think back. OMG it was a riot and made the national news. I look around, assessing the risks for this year. The young Head makes a beeline for us. Her tattoos and piercings speak volumes about how education has leapt forward over the decades.

"So glad you could come," she gushes, giving me what I would describe as the once over. "I've changed the format," she says. "I open the gathering with the usual welcome and do a roll call of those who cannot be with us but I don't give details about their passings. It's too distressing for the more fragile old girls." Her eyes drift over to Deirdre. "I then speak about our successes but it's directed at the younger old girls." She coughs. "Oh! I don't mean to be ageist, I know success can transcend age, but you know what I mean." She goes on. "We've got an Olympic bronze medallist this year. She learnt the high jump on our sports fields in 2013. The accident she had enabled her to enter the Paralympics." She almost looks proud, as it the accident was a school accolade.

She tells us that there will be no tour of the school, which was abandoned in 2006 after that trigger. Maybe she doesn't know it was me who lost it that day. Well, my appearance has changed and she would only have seen an old photo and the YouTube video. Since then, I've changed my mousy look to one fashioned on the beautiful Nina Alu – Mrs Iggy Pop.

I think back to the trigger. It was the sight of Miss Cunliffe that tipped me over and the smell of the Domestic Science room. The room had been modernised since her day. The old cookers and flat irons were gone but the bench was the same, and the mixing bowls. And the rolling pin. Oh, the rolling pin . . .

"I did not wield it! It rolled over." I recall lines from my Statement . . . It rolled off the table and Miss Cunliffe tried to retrieve it with her foot – the lace on her brogue got caught and she took off like she was on a skateboard. For a moment she looked quite majestic, her hair flying as she crossed the room and did a Flip Trick followed by a Chinese Nollie. The fall was inevitable. The review in Sidewalk UK explained where Miss C. had gone wrong.

The Multiple Flip rotation down the stairs was worse and lead to the inevitable. There was a lot of blood. Paramedics did their best but it was curtains – curtains for Miss Cunliffe.

At least she was a good age. At a hundred and three, she'd outlived many of her girls – as she called us. And if she could have chosen a place to end her days, it would have been in her domain. Her Heaven, as we learnt she called it, at her memorial. Shame really that she had moved beyond her Heaven out into the corridor and down the stairs.

I'm brought back to the present. The Head is waxing lyrical about the Paralympian and she is passing a large bouquet to Deirdre to do the presentation. Deirdre then takes to the stage and gives a rendition of the old school song. In perfect pitch and with a touch of Susan Boyle. The lime green dress doesn't look too bad now.

We learn later that Deirdre is actually very ill. A brain tumour, someone says.

"God, life's a bitch," you say, as we leave.

Born in a Hut

Terence Brand

Joel Smith stood in the small church's porch, holding his black top hat to the chest of his morning coat as he watched the congregation file in. The ushers were doing well, herding the punters to their pews. That was the first hurdle to cross – get everyone settled without any unseemly arguments and lethally brandished umbrellas.

"No, no – Uncle Dick and Auntie Fanny haven't spoken since the last funeral. No, I don't care if they've been married for fifty years – you can't put them together, there'll be murder done, and you wouldn't want that in church, would you?"

Joel sighed. People didn't appreciate the snags of a Funeral Director's job. Everything had to go like clockwork. The last place for a slip up, certainly a murder, was in church. And today of all days, he needed to get this ceremony done and dusted and these plebs away to their "See-the-Old-Bastard-Off" party. Well, you could hardly say wake – they were holding the bash in the billiard hall, weren't they?

Sounds of traffic in the quiet cul-de-sac interrupted Joel's musings. He looked across the churchyard. The second cortege of the morning was arriving. A shiny hearse carrying a coffin bedecked in flowers. Joel checked his watch. Only a tad early. Still, Rolls-Royces and Bentleys were already arriving for the elaborate service that was to follow Albert Warren's interment.

Should he speak to the vicar? Ask him to hurry the first ceremony along? Put Albert in his hole and clear the decks. Couldn't have his lot hanging around, could he? Mustn't risk mixing the hoi polloi with the gentry. Absolutely not!

Stifling a shudder, Joel examined the occupants of the front pews. When was that motley bunch last in church? Most were only there to make sure old Albert Warren really had popped his clogs.

Ah, the vicar was on the ball – here comes the coffin. Typical – the four bruisers bouncing it on their shoulders looked exactly like what they were – the local bin men. You'd think they were taking the old fellow down to the tip.

Hallo – something wasn't right. Why was everyone nudging each other and whispering? Some of the so-and-sos were grinning!

It was the coffin, wasn't it? A large mahogany affair dripping with brass. Who among the Warrens could have afforded that? More to the point, who'd have bothered?

A devastating revelation leapt into Joel's head – a picture of the plain pine box sitting in the old Austin hearse parked at the back of the church.

Oh, no – they couldn't have.

But they bloody had, hadn't they?

Jamming his top hat on his head, Joel dashed out of the church. Dodging an usher urging the gentry to remain in their cars, he ran round the back. Yes, there were the two hearses, side by side. And there was Albert in his pine box. Waiting serenely in the back of his last earthly transport. Going nowhere – certainly not to his grave.

Taking a deep breath, Joel forced himself to think rationally. What to do?

The sight of the church's gravediggers leaning on their shovels beside two newly dug holes gave hope. He ran over. "George, Fred – I need help."

George, a stoic sixty year old, merely stared. Fred, younger and faster, said, "Why, what's up, Mr Smith?"

Joel quickly explained. "So, you see," he concluded as the brass-bound coffin and its mourners appeared around the corner, "when the Warrens have gone, I want you to lift the big coffin out and put Albert in. Then the big coffin goes back into the big hearse. Okay?"

He turned away only to halt when George called, "Aren't you helping, Mr Smith?"

Joel shook his head. "I'll keep the Buddley-Harringtons busy while you make the swap."

Back in the church, the new congregation was getting restless. Lady Grace was airing her displeasure. "My Stammy would never have stood for such incompetence. A self-made man, was my Stammy. Born in a wooden hut. Proud of it – proud of it, I say! Pulled himself up by his bootstraps. Made a million before he was thirty. He'd never have allowed anyone to treat him like this."

At last, Sir Stamford Buddley-Harrington's coffin made its second entrance, majestically and sedately. The moment was in danger of being spoilt by the clods of earth dropping onto the church's floor. Joel gestured. An usher crawled behind with a dustpan and brush, discreetly gathering the deposits.

The ceremony went with no more hitches. Sir Stamford duly interred, his mourners climbed aboard their limousines to be driven off to the Grand Hotel. Wiping sweat from his brow, Joel Smith joined George and Fred by the holes.

The two were wide-eyed. Fred explained. "The funeral parlour got it wrong, Mr Smith. While we were heaving the fancy coffin out, the lid came off. It weren't Sir Stamford – it were Albert!"

"Typical Albert," George declared. "If he fell in a sewer, he'd come out with his pockets full of brass!"

"That's right," Fred chuckled. "We didn't have time to make a swap – you want us to do it now?"

Joel could still hear Lady Grace. "Born in a hut. Proud of it!"

"No," he said. "Leave Stammy in the cheap wooden box. I'm sure he feels at home."

Letters Regarding an Internal Matter

John Rudkin

Letter to Rev J Thompson, found by him left on the desk in his study at 9.00 a.m.

Monday 13th May 2013.

Dear Rev Thompson,

After perusing a letter that you carelessly left on our desk I understand that Dr Emery, your psychiatrist, has finally confirmed in writing that there is nothing, physically or mentally wrong with you. That my very existence is nothing more than your imagination running riot, due to a sleeping disorder which has since cleared up of its own accord.

I now, therefore, feel the time is right to introduce new rules regarding the joint use of the single body that we share. Friday, Saturday and Sunday nights will now be for my personal use only. You will have sole occupation on work days. I realise that regarding Sundays I will not take possession until after evensong. I must insist that you don't waste my time chin-wagging with those imbeciles you refer to as "your flock", around the lych-gate, as you have been wont to do in the past. I have also decided to continue to allow you specific private occupancy on Thursday evenings, your weekly dart-playing night, subject to you monitoring your alcohol intake on these occasions. I have found that on Fridays, in the past, I have had to put up with the remnants of a hangover. The ladies in the red-light district have also complained of my beery breath and I'm having to take the blame for something I am not responsible for. You know, for a clergyman you really are a selfish bastard.

Now for the change that will improve our complicated lives. As the star act in our duo, now that our special problem is back between ourselves only, I must inform you that it would be better if I became the "main man" and you got used to being the alter ego. I would wish this to begin immediately of course.

I see no reason for any argument as to the implementation of these new rules and I refuse to have any truck with petty complaints from a *minor* partner. I therefore expect you to adopt the new regime as of now.

Yours partially,

"Big" John Strong

Big John

Letter to "Big John" found by him in the same place that he left his letter to Rev J Thompson, 8.00 p.m.

Friday 17th May 2013.

Dear John,

First of all, may I congratulate you on finding a method of contacting me. We have never met and never can; when either of us has possession of the mantle of flesh, the other floats around in the ether, somewhere. By writing letters when one has the hands to do so and then leaving them to be read when the recipient has eyes to read with is a stroke of genius. Well done.

However, I find the content of your missive rude, overbearing and despicable. May I remind you that until I reached adulthood, my body was mine alone. Around the time of my twenty-first birthday *you* barged in and tried to take charge, thus causing me great upset.

Some people tend to think peace-loving priests are timid and perhaps even a little cowardly. I can assure you that that is not a description that could be applied to me.

You may, foolishly, consider yourself to have the stronger personality. You may also feel that there is nothing I can do to stop your takeover bid. Consider this, then. It is Friday evening at 8.00 p.m.. This being exactly the time that I vacate the body and you enter, at the last second I leap in front of a moving bus. The pain, trouble and misery are all yours now and during the night you experience a lingering death. Yes, I pass away too . . . but painlessly and peacefully. Your master Satan has you all to himself, now. I, on the other hand, am with the Lord.

This scenario is just a possibility. I won't be making any such move without many hours of thought and prayer, of course. So,

John, I say things stay as they are. If you still wish to push ahead with your new rules, please write again first.

One last thing: your very being has proved to me the existence of the soul. I thank you for that.

God bless you.

Your co-tenant,

John Thompson

John Thompson

Reader please note:
Rev John Thompson died peacefully in his bed at precisely 7.55 p.m. on Friday 13 July 2018. No further correspondence had passed between the two men after the above letter, written some five years before.

Drop Dead Gorgeous

Suzanne Conboy Hill

I first met Dillon when my dead gran tripped me up in front of him. There was me, meandering along the seafront watching small dogs on extending leads crochet themselves into yapping compounds each time they encountered others of their ilk; and there was he, arrowing through them, the sleek lycra-ed warp to their woof. I was OK but he landed up in hospital with several broken bones and his bike was a write-off. Gran beamed like it was her birthday and she'd knocked back her celebratory bottle of whisky all in one go.

I wasn't planning on visiting him; after all, he'd reason to be mad and maybe even to monetise that. Can you sue pedestrians? But Gran had other ideas; I got the train to uni, it broke down and the replacement bus dropped me outside the hospital. I walked. There was an incident and a diversion that went right past A&E. I tried taking a taxi; the driver had a heart attack. So to avoid any further disasters befalling the largely innocent public, I gave in. Five minutes tops should do it, I reckoned.

"Okay, I'll go," I said. "But I don't need an audience, right?"

Fat chance.

"Lovely, innee?" Gran said, breathing pickle fumes over my shoulder.

"Shut up," I said, trying not to move my mouth as if this somehow compensated for the conspicuous absence of a third party. It didn't. Dillon looked around the room and started to reach for the call bell. I could see his point.

"No, not you," I said, and fiddled around with a fantasy earpiece under my hair. "Bloody signal's gone," I said, palming the non-existent device and shoving it in my pocket. I gave him one of those *modern technology, what can you do?* looks and shrugged.

Gran continued her onslaught. "Physicist," she said, picking at teeth that would be at least a hundred years old if she'd managed to haul her liver past 86. "Should suit you, with all your book-learnin' an' that." She gave me a shove. "Go on, sit on his bed." I was propelled forwards and alarm spread across Dillon's face as the woman who had put him there in the first place threatened to flatten him all over again. I grabbed at a drip pole. It was on wheels so we took each other down, along with a vase of flowers, a jug of water, and a box of tissues. The almighty racket drew the attention of a frosty-looking nurse in pink scrubs who rushed first to Dillon to inspect him for injury, and then turned her rather less solicitous gaze on me, sprawled on the floor at her feet.

"And you are?" she said, like we were at a posh party and I wasn't on the guest list. I opened my mouth preparing to kill two birds with one F-bomb but . . .

"My girlfriend," said Dillon, into the gap.

"What?"

"Yes," Gran said through my teeth, tittering in my ear and making kissy-kissy noises.

The nurse glared at me, then at Dillon. "Well, in that case . . ." She stomped away to find a cleaner she could terrorise.

"Jeez!" Dillon said, rolling his eyes. "I owe you; bloody woman's been ogling me since I got here. Never seems to be off duty. Have you seen that Stephen King film?" He smiled one of those crooked smiles you read about.

"Look look look!" Gran whickered at me. "Drop dead gorgeous!"

I cocked an appraising eye. "Well, actually . . ."

"You saw it, the movie?"

"No, I meant – anyway, how are you?"

He told me.

We laughed.

I stayed two hours.

I promised to pick him up and take him home when he was discharged, and cook dinner as he couldn't use his hands that well. Turned out he could. Whole other story.

I moved in.

Gran stayed away for quite a while, probably to focus on another deviant descendant, then suddenly, back she came.

"Cheating gigolo," she announced from behind the sofa. I nearly lost my takeaway. "Quantum research shove-it-up-your-jacksie conference, my Aunt Fanny," she said. Gran liked an expletive or two, albeit somewhat retro ones.

"What do you mean?"

"So-called research assistant – more bosom than brains," she said.

"And the bosom's not much to write home about, if you ask me."

Gran was right; Rihanna, her name was, and I met her at the faculty Christmas do a couple of months later. There she was, goggling at Dillon, passing him wine and nibbles, chirping about quantum entangled whatnots and superstring that apparently has toes, and Dillon mesmerised by her heaving chest. Gran dug me in the ribs then grabbed both my ears. This, apparently, was a way of establishing a conduit between her plane of existence and ours. She shrieked at Dillon, "You cunning, conniving, slippery little wormhole, you!" Then she rose into the air and loomed over Rihanna. "And you should know all about quantum, with your itty bitty IQ and your Schrödinger's now-you-see-it-now-you-don't brazz-ee-ere!" Gran had evidently upgraded her vocabulary since our last encounter; she embarked on a cackle.

Then somebody with a beard that looked as though it might house a decent-sized lunch, and a T-shirt bearing the periodic table in swearwords, said, 'Quantum phasing,' in hushed tones like he was in a church. He gawped, simultaneously awestruck and terrified, and Gran turned on him, treated him to a blast of old onions and fried liver right into his face. She clacked her teeth.

"Phantom," she hissed, and hovered yellow fingers over his throat.

"Cobblers," said Dillon. "No such thing as ghosts. Quantum phased reality shifts though, there's mileage in that." His face went into intellectually distracted mode. It was short-lived.

Gran loomed back in Dillon's direction, "Quantum reality shift, my arse," she said. "Tell you what, though, let's put it to the test." And she dropped the ceiling on him.

Some days it's just Dillon sitting behind me on the train, sometimes it's Gran; other times it's the pair of them. They're still arguing the toss about ghosts versus quantum universes and they can't agree on suitable boyfriends for me, which threatens the long-term survival of potential suitors. So Gran borrowed me a part-time dog for company. "Big bugger," she said, handing me his collar. "And he's got what you might call ongoing duties elsewhere, but he'll keep the riff-raff away; happy clappies, dodgy roofers, Tories."

He is and he does because he's got one helluva howl on him, but he's a poppet and when all three of us are indoors together, we each have a head to pat.

Let Sleeping Dogs Lie

Sue Ajax-Lewis

Ferret was standing in the queue behind Mrs Postlethwaite, waiting to cash his unemployment benefit. Of course, Ferret wasn't the name on the slip, but he had always been known as Ferret. It was partly because of his long sharp nose, but mostly because of his unerring ability to sniff out any opportunity that might benefit him without any great effort on his own part.

He glanced casually around the post office, wondering if the CCTV cameras were trained on him or whether he could quickly pocket anything to top up his benefit. It was not, he assured himself, enough to benefit him at all, really; certainly not in the manner to which he would like to become accustomed.

Mrs Postlethwaite, meanwhile, had discovered a friend directly in front of her in the queue and was whiling away their wait for their pensions by a bit of a gossip. Ferret was obliged to listen. He couldn't help it, being in such close proximity.

Just his luck; not only to have to waste time queueing but also to have to listen to this waffle on top. He eyed the backs of Mrs Postlethwaite's and Mrs Absolom's heads with undisguised exasperation and impatience.

"Yes, I am just having a bit of a clear out," Mrs Postlethwaite was saying to her friend. "You know, giving a few bits and bobs to the charity shop. They might do someone some good. I'm going to let them have that old fur coat he bought me all those years ago. Do you know, I never wanted one? I'd rather have had a nice navy wool one but he was so keen to show everyone he could afford to buy his wife a proper fur coat. I hadn't the heart to tell him. I never did like wearing it; I looked like a Himalayan bear because it was a long dark brown thing. I'll be glad to see the back of it. Now he's bedridden, he'll never know and it'll keep somebody warm."

"If they don't mind looking like a bear," said Mrs Absolom and they giggled old lady giggles and nudged each other.

Behind them, Ferret threw his eyes up to the ceiling and sighed heavily with increased impatience.

"I'm going to pile everything in the hall," went on Mrs Postlethwaite. "They're coming to pick it up because you know we don't have a car anymore and I can't carry it all that way. I've told them to come after four because I've got to nip out and see the doctor at three and it takes me a while to get there and back nowadays."

She leant heavily on her walking stick and sighed wistfully.

"But, you know, I don't like to go out and leave Peter twice in one day. He does hate it when I'm not there. And, bless him, he gets so excited when we have company; he really loves visitors. Still, I'll be as quick as I can. Don't want them to have a wasted trip because there's no one to let them in if I'm out."

Behind them in the queue, Ferret's wandering thoughts snapped to attention.

He was suddenly all ears and his nose was twitching.

If her husband was bedridden in one room and she was going to see the doctor at three, the house would be left virtually unguarded. He would bet his life there would be no burglar alarm and he could probably slip the lock without too much bother and have a quiet look round while she was out. Suddenly, Ferret felt a lot better. This wait in the post office might be a bit more profitable than he had been expecting.

So when Mrs. Postlethwaite left the post office, Ferret wasn't far behind her.

He had to feign interest in all sorts of shop windows to avoid catching up with her because she was so slow. He loitered outside McDonalds, pretending to read the menu. He bent down retying shoelaces on his trainers that didn't need retying. He sat for a few minutes on a bench at a bus stop, hands in his pockets, whistling. Never once was Mrs Postlethwaite out of his sight.

Eventually, his vigilance was rewarded and he saw her turn in at the gate of an old fashioned semi-detached bungalow in a quiet road.

He left her time to get in and close the front door then he crossed the road and sauntered slowly past on the other side, glancing casually at the bungalow as he did and noting, as expected and with relief, that there was no evidence of any alarm system.

Built probably mid-thirties, with nice thick brick walls which would mask any sound he might make. Not like the paper-thin walls in modern places where you had to tiptoe the whole time. Even the front door was contained inside a helpful brick porch.

And just across the road was a bus stop with a proper shelter and not just a bench. Ferret was beginning to like this opportunity more and more.

He pretended to post something in the pillar box on his side of the road then walked slowly back the way he had come.

He glanced at his watch. Twelve thirty. So he had about two hours before she would leave to see the doctor at three. OK. He would go to the pub and have a pint.

Just as well he had worn his trainers today. Ferret always wore his trainers whenever he might get up to something, just in case he had to make a quick getaway. It made running so much easier. He had learnt that lesson when one of his mates had tried to mug an old lady wearing his new boots and had tripped himself up with his own Cuban heels.

Just after two thirty, Ferret arrived back at the bus shelter with a copy of a paper that he had acquired from the pub when its owner had gone to the gents'. He settled himself in the corner, apparently immersed in the sports pages but not so immersed that he didn't see Mrs Postlethwaite coming out of her front door.

She paused halfway out of the porch and, holding the door ajar, called back, "Goodbye Peter, I won't be long." Then she closed it behind her and hobbled down the path, leaning heavily on her stick.

"Come on, come on, shake a leg," Ferret muttered to her, under his breath.

He waited until she had turned the corner and then, without haste, dropped the paper, ground out his cigarette and sauntered across the road.

He walked casually up the path to the blue front door. It gave straightaway to the practised slice of his stolen supermarket reward card against the cheap lock and he slid quickly inside.

In a dark corner of the gloomy hall appeared to be the pile of things left out for the charity shop, apparently covered by the dark thick Himalayan-bear-like fur coat. Ferret gave it an experimental poke with his foot and then turned away. He wasn't interested in old tat left out for charity. In any case, fur didn't fetch anything these days, what with the animal rights lot sounding off about it.

He slipped silently into the lounge, easing the door to carefully behind him, so as not to make any noise and alert the bedridden old boy.

There was a sideboard that might yield something. That was usually where old people kept any bits of valuables that they might still have, didn't they?

He pulled open the drawers and began to search through them. Nothing in that one.

Ferret tutted. He was so engrossed in his search that he failed to notice the door being pushed open slowly behind him.

The sleepy old man in his bedroom thought he heard a muffled scream from the adjacent lounge. "Marjorie?" he called, but he knew she had gone out to see the doctor. He continued to listen but heard nothing more.

Perhaps it was kids playing outside, he wondered, or next door's telly. Or maybe he was dozing and had imagined it? Deafness could do that sometimes. He would have a snooze until Marjorie came back from the doctor's. She would bring him a nice cup of tea and a piece of cake and they could chat about her day. Contented, he closed his eyes and went back to sleep.

Mrs Postlethwaite let herself in through her front door. "Peter?" she called, "I'm back."

She looked at her watch. Ooh, the charity people would be here soon. She must collect up everything and put it by the front door ready for them, especially that blessed Himalayan-bear-like fur coat.

Mrs Postlethwaite hobbled into her lounge. Stopped short. And gasped.

Peter looked round happily. Bless him; he got so excited when they had company. He really loved visitors.

Squashed flat underneath twelve stone of slobbering smelly old Newfoundland dog, a terrified Ferret was slowly being licked to death.

Rabbit Pie

Patricia Feinberg-Stoner

I relied on the rabbit.

It is, after all, my signature autumn dish. Fragrant with herbs and wine, the flesh moist and succulent, with the sweet-sharp surprise of mushrooms lightly sautéed in butter, rosemary and lemon juice and added at the last moment to the savoury stew. I always relied on the rabbit. Whenever I wanted a favour. Whenever I wanted a man. And the rabbit never let me down.

That's how I got Drew in the first place. I spotted him in the library, with his clutch of Delias and Marguerite Pattens. Drew with his easy swagger, his heart-catching grin. Tall and gangling with an unruly mop of sandy hair and owlish spectacles.

Handsome Drew. Drew the bastard.

"Do you like cooking?" I asked companionably as we waited for the machine to check our books out.

"Yes, I do. My real passion is game, but the library seems to be a bit thin on the ground in that department," he said. There was a hint of Geordie in his accent.

"Oh, I know a wonderful book for game cookery," I enthused and – dear reader, I confess it! - I batted my eyelashes. "It's called *The Sporting Wife*. It's quite old, and probably out of print now, but I'm sure the library could find you a copy. What's your favourite?"

"I like pheasant and I adore grouse, and I've got a really great recipe from my grandmother – she was French – for quails cooked with oranges. But I've never had any luck cooking rabbit. It always comes out dry, with far too many fiddly bones."

I sent up a prayer of thanks to whichever saint was on my case that day. I confided modestly, "I make a mean rabbit pie . . ."

And of course one thing led to another.

I have a special touch with rabbit. Finding the right beast is essential. Forget your supermarket junk or – heaven forbid – that so-called Chinese rabbit. It's probably cat. No: I usually make the trek to the New Forest to go to Seal's in Lymington. They're the best game butchers I know, and if I smile sweetly, Adam (the boss) will skin and joint the rabbit for me. Next comes the preparation. Trim the leg pieces and carefully ease the flesh from the ribs. Too many people cook the whole rabbit, and then spend the meal digging bits of bone out of their mouths.

Slather the meat with mustard (I use my favourite tarragon-infused Dijon), then put it in a deep dish with a couple of sprigs of rosemary, some cloves of garlic, juniper berries and bay leaves. (Now make a note of those berries and bay leaves, you'll see why in a minute.) Pour a whole bottle of good red wine over the rabbit – I tend to favour a rich burgundy – and leave to marinate in a cool place (NOT the fridge!) for at least 24 hours.

Put the rabbit in a low oven, and once it has cooked long and slow – allow at least an hour and a half – you can toss in the mushrooms and taste for seasoning. Now comes the clever bit. Take the meat out with a slotted spoon and put it into individual oven dishes. Reduce the cooking liquid by half so it is really rich, and spoon it over the rabbit.

I don't use pastry, which tends to go soggy. Instead, I cover each dish with finely sliced par-boiled potatoes, dusted with salt and pepper and dotted with butter. When it comes out of the oven, the underside of the potato is tender with the rich juices and the top is crisp, golden and beginning to curl at the edges.

I pulled out all the stops, the first time Drew came to dinner. Though I say it myself, the meal was a triumph. As a little extra touch, I wrote his initial and mine in paprika on the two dishes – "D" and "A". It made him smile. I do it every time, now, it's our little joke.

It was lovely for a while. Drew and I got on really well in the kitchen and in bed – what more could a woman want? But after a few months, there were those telltale signs. He wasn't as punctual as he used to be. His kisses were distracted and he forgot to praise my cooking. I knew something was wrong.

I'd heard a lot about Francesca. She was an apprentice in the architect's studio Drew owned with his brother. Francesca was so gifted. Francesca had such flair. The client really liked the drawings Francesca did. Francesca this, Francesca that . . .

He swore she was just a bright pupil, meant nothing to him. And, poor fool, I believed him. Until the day I was walking past my favourite restaurant, The Game Pie. Our restaurant. And there they were in the window, cosy as you please, holding hands across – I couldn't believe my eyes – a plate of rabbit pie.

So here I am again, cooking my special rabbit dish for Drew.

My special rabbit dish, with just a little extra. The laburnum bush in my garden is past its glory now, but the seed heads are forming, and the leaves look so like bay leaves when they are chopped up. Anyone could make a mistake. Laburnum poisoning can be fatal, I hear. Ah, well.

The meat is melting from two hours in a low oven. Carefully I spoon it into the dishes. Carefully, I fold a few seeds – are they juniper or laburnum, I wonder – into one of the dishes. Carefully I sprinkle some chopped bay leaves on top. At least, I think they are bay leaves . . .

The sauce is thickened and aromatic, you wouldn't notice any slight bitterness. I slice the potatoes over the two dishes and reach for the paprika.

The phone rings. My heart stops: is he going to cancel? His voice sounds serious as he says, "Amanda, I have to talk to you. Do you mind if I come up early, say in half an hour?"

Panic stations. I'd better get those rabbit pies in the oven quick sharp. What if he decides to have his little chat and then leave without eating?

Now I'm standing here like a lemon, looking at two absolutely identical dishes. In my rush to get them in the oven I forgot to initial them.

The doorbell is ringing.

Mrs Green's Adventure

Jackie Harvey

"Well thank you, Mrs Green, I think that's all we need from you at the moment." The Police Sergeant closed his notebook. "Of course, if you think of anything else to help us with our enquiries, please let us know." He smiled sympathetically at the frail, grey-haired lady sitting in her armchair, a tartan blanket covering her knees. "Are you sure there is no one we can contact to help you? It must have been a shock."

"No, thank you, I'll be fine." She smiled. "I have Willow here to keep me company, but thanks for your help." She gestured with her aged, wrinkly hand and reached down to stroke Willow, her black Labrador, sitting by her side.

After the policeman had left, she sat for a while contemplating her next move. Yesterday, coming home to find her back door open and muddy footprints over the kitchen floor, she'd phoned the police. They'd arrived and searched the premises but found nothing and she agreed nothing had been taken. Nothing she'd tell them about anyway.

I'll have a cup of tea and think what's best to do. It had been an enormous shock but she'd handled it well and sorted the problem herself. *I don't want to bother the family, they'll only tell me to go and stay with them.*

No, she didn't want that. She loved her independence and had always managed to cope. But her life had been so dull recently, since the loss of her best friend Beryl. They'd had so many adventures together over the years of their friendship. Yes, that's what she needed: a bit of an adventure. Now she knew what to do.

Flinging off the blanket, she spoke to Willow: "Right old girl, think it's time for a bit of fun." After collecting the key to the cellar from the kitchen, she opened the basement door, flicked on the light switch and carefully descended the steep steps. Willow raced ahead, sniffing at everything. She stopped abruptly and barked at an old dirty blanket lying in the far corner, shrouded in shadow.

Hesitantly, the woman reached the bottom step. "Willow

59

leave," she shouted, moving towards the darkened corner, where she kicked at the blanket.

"Ah there you are," she spoke patronisingly to the curled up figure, "just where I left you yesterday." Two eyes peered at her from beneath the blanket. She continued more forcefully. "Now listen carefully. The police have just left." She moved closer, noticing the familiar caked mud on the figure's trainers. "So, you will tell me where you've hidden the jewellery and money." She raised her voice. "If you don't do as I say, I'll call the police back and tell them you returned and I've caught you." She kicked the figure again. "It may not be my money or jewellery, but only you and I know that, so I suggest you be clever." She paused. "I don't see you've much of an option really, do you?" She waited. "So, what's it to be?"

Willow sat beside here waiting. The only sound was the gurgling of the central heating pipes. Or was it coming from the curled up figure?

Consecutive

Derek McMillan

For a forest, the Ashdown Forest is remarkably free of trees. Consequently it used to be a great place to take Barker for a run. It's more of a sedate walk these days. Except, that is, on the 9th of September, when he suddenly went haring off as though he had spotted a Woofums dog treat going begging.

We followed at our own pace to find him scrabbling away like a demented beagle, strange behaviour because he is a German Shepherd/Alsatian.

"What is it, Barker?" I asked politely.

Suddenly we could see what it was. Somebody had hurriedly buried a box and Barker had just as hurriedly unburied it.

We opened the box. It contained a lot of money.

Any decent upright citizens would have reported this to the police but we couldn't because on the 9th of September the police were on strike. They were protesting against cuts in the budget. The strike was short-lived; the Police Federation did not have a strike fund. The cuts, however, were long-lived, as one wag in the newspapers put it, "The magic money tree is suffering from dutch elm disease." Public services were in tatters and the social fabric of the country with them. It was more or less voluntary to go to prison for a crime; it was pot luck if you got a hospital appointment for an urgent case.

Micah didn't estimate the money in the box at £500,000 in twenty pound notes. She actually counted it and she found something else out.

"A batch of forged notes often have the same serial number or a limited set of serial numbers."

"And these are different?" I asked.

"Consecutive. I checked."

"Half a million pounds of government money has just gone missing," the BBC News announced. "This is not an accounting error. The money is in cash and the serial numbers of the notes are being circulated."

"Ministers' Missing Millions" was the headline in more than

one newspaper, sacrificing accuracy for alliteration.

Micah used a Tor browser, which apparently "hid her IP address", whatever that is. She sent a one-word message to the Bank of England and received a one-word reply almost instantly.

Her message was "Consecutive."

The reply was "WhatsApp".

WhatsApp is a thing which uses end-to-end encryption (your guess is as good as mine) but the upshot is that state agencies and other interested parties cannot eavesdrop on your conversation.

She duly contacted the Bank employee with the aforesaid app and I was able to watch their conversation.

She began with the first serial number and then the final one.

"The numbers are consecutive and the box was found in the Ashdown Forest."

"Thank you for your communication."

There was a pause.

"If you value your life and liberty, I suggest you are not the person who found the box."

"This conversation is at an end."

"What do you think about that, Craig?"

"A bit rude."

"Yes. Apart from that."

Micah likes lists so I responded: "A) They did not want the money found. B) they did not want it found by us but by another party. C) They are up to something."

"Yes, Craig, but surely the Bank of England is never 'up to something' without the backing of powerful allies."

"Money is never transported in cash, not half a million. That is suspicious in itself," I said.

"So why were they transporting such a sum in cash? Why did they not want anybody to find it?"

"And why has that car been parked across the road for the past three hours?"

We drew the curtains. They are quite nice and we thought chummy in the vehicle could take photographs of them instead of us.

We had ID with the word "Police" in large letters and smaller letters explaining we were not police officers but aiding with technical work. I didn't think this would fool our new friend for a moment.

"Let's invite Joanne to dinner," Micah suggested. Sergeant Joanne Thallman was not only a good friend but also a genuine police officer.

"Actually we have an interesting situation here. We have had a man sitting across the road in a blue Peugeot 207" She gave the registration number. "He's been there for a couple of hours now and shows no sign of shifting."

"And you'd like me to have a word?"

"If that is OK."

"Is Craig making his lasagne?"

"Yes."

"We have a deal."

Joanne came with her partner, DC Janet Small, and a bottle of Casillero Del Diablo Merlot.

"I had no luck with your new friend. I can't tell you if he was with Special Branch or anything."

That was all we needed to know.

Joanne and Janet were always good company.

We spent most of the evening talking about "The Crown" but their unease about the state of the nation crept in to the conversation.

"We were on the picket line while old Ben Tillotson was in his office. Of course, he had sod all to do with all his minions on strike. And the Federation were not pleased with him, not pleased at all."

"The lunatic drivers, the pavement parkers and the burglars have always had an easy time of it because of shortage of what they still call 'manpower', but now things are worse," said Joanne.

"Overworked and underpaid," Janet chipped in.

"A bit like teachers?" Micah couldn't resist adding.

"But at least your union has a strike fund and some idea about how to run a strike," said Joanne.

Then we steered the conversation back to the TV we all enjoyed.

The evening ended all too soon and we said our goodbyes. The man in the Peugeot was still there as our guests were leaving. We waved at him.

Quaintly, Micah detected that the powers that be had bugged our telephone. Micah found this hilarious. I thought it was a violation of blah blah blah.

In an apparent diversion, Micah told a story. "A prominent leftist in the 1960s had a conversation with a friend in Liverpool. After the conversation there was a click and then he was surprised to hear the whole conversation played back to him."

"A mistake?"

"And I'm the Queen of Sheba. No, the intention was to intimidate. The result was that from then on leftists abandoned the telephone as a means of communication. Things like encryption and WhatsApp made that possible."

She nodded towards the box.

"This money might as well be counterfeit for all the use it is. Nobody can spend as much as one note without the police coming down on them like a ton of bricks. Before you ask, we can't give it to charity because then the charity would fall under suspicion."

However the money was serving one purpose. The BBC made that clear.

"The government is facing a backbench rebellion over what is being called the million pound scandal. Over to our parliamentary correspondent."

"The sum of money is small compared to the sort of sums ministers spend or squander on a regular basis. If I may correct you, it is not a million pounds it is half a million, but it has vanished without trace. There is usually an explanation when government money goes missing. There is none."

"Here at Westminster, there is wild speculation about what they were proposing to do with this money. Everything from paying off gangsters to bribing foreign potentates has been suggested. The less the backbenchers have in the way of hard fact, the more there is in terms of conspiracy theories."

The BBC has a summary of the morning papers which means we don't have to buy more than one paper. Every paper had a different theory about the "missing millions" and there were various culprits. The most far-fetched was that it was for a drug deal. I can't imagine the Prime Minister's habit was that far advanced.

"And they are saying it is to organise a militia to attack Parliament," said Micah. "The only problem is that the ruling party is the one with a majority in Parliament, so it would be unlikely for the government to organise a Trump-style riot against themselves."

The papers are calling for the Home Secretary or the Chancellor of the Exchequer to resign.

By the midday news, the pair of them had offered to resign and their resignations had been declined.

That evening we had a visitor. He gave his name but as it turned out to be an alias I won't mention it.

"I need a word with you, son."

I am 69, nobody calls me "son" unless they are trying to be irritating. Once I realised he was trying to annoy, he lost his vexing licence.

"You want a word with us," I said.

Micah joined us over his protests.

"Look, love I just want a wee word with Craig here."

She smiled sweetly and took a seat. I don't think she offers tea to people who call her "love".

"Phones," he said in a peremptory tone which was part of his bothersome brat image.

We put the phones on the table. He switched them off and put a smart gadget alongside them.

"No other recording devices in the room," he said, half to himself.

"Craig, Mr McLairy, I am not authorised to tell you anything, let alone your good lady here."

"That could be a problem, given what you are going to tell us to do," said Micah.

He did a double take at that.

"What makes you think . . ."

"My brain, usually. Tell us what you want us to do. Then tell us why."

When he remained silent she added, "Or we could talk to your superior. If you can't tell us, perhaps she can."

That was too much for him. "Is there any chance of a cup of tea?"

"Certainly, Craig can you do me one, too?"

I made three teas and we settled down to a more amicable chat.

He looked straight at Micah this time.

"You know why the money was where you found it."

She nodded.

"What do you think of the state of the country right now?"

"A pig's ear?"

He visibly relaxed.

"And you want to do something about it?"

We nodded.

"The intention was that the money would go missing and not be found by anybody, least of all people like you. The disposal of the money was subcontracted and the subcontractors made a mess of it. You can put that right."

He made a suggestion and we listened carefully.

He stayed in the house and I went out and got in the car. I was carrying a very large parcel. This left our special friend with a dilemma: should he stay or should he go?

When I reached the end of the street, it was clear he had decided to follow me. I went to Arundel and waited for my tail to catch up. I went into the cathedral carrying my parcel. When I prayed, he was two pews behind me.

I then took the parcel to a charity shop. He tore in as soon as I had left. I hope he is happy with my old clothes.

Meanwhile, Micah had a very expensive bonfire in the back garden and carefully broke up the ashes as per instructions. The missing half million was truly missing now.

The next day, the newspapers were suspiciously unanimous in demanding the resignation of the Prime Minister.

"That doesn't mean it will happen," Micah said.

But it did, the next day.

"He will go to his grave wondering what happened to the money," said Micah.

Very probably.

Jazz City

Jacqui Rozdoba

Her blood sings with the rhythms of an evening of jazz, as the door swings open to offer life on the street and the last of late summer warmth. She turns towards Soho Square to brush the shadow puppets of animators, artists, and punters whose hands held pencils and clutched sticky glasses in bars long gone.

She sidles invisibly down Frith Street, passing neat young men in shiny grey suits bearing bleached white smiles and a sense of entitlement, then glides through Chinatown, around bunches of girls, falling in and out of sculpted poses, in and out of skimpy dresses, in and out of love. She hurries on through the spiced night air to Charing Cross.

Judging the lights, a sprint to catch the last train. She collapses, with a self-satisfied smile, onto the middle of three seats, closing her eyes to focus on catching her breath. As the train pulls out, she opens them to see two middle-aged men in the window seats. They lean across, dance round each other with sighs and nods, eyes darting, firing flirting glances. Eager to share iphone photos, gestures becoming grander, movements more intense, feet step out and arms entwine.

The dance so entrances, she could have missed her station, had not so many people emptied onto the platform. The clock tower, visible from the bus stop, merely fringes the market. Once a symbol of civic power, it is now overshadowed by slabs of new building that block the sky, monuments to a new global order.

The bus arrives to pull her out of the biting wind. A Babel of voices. She's lucky to get on at all. It is already morning, much too early, and much too late for a bus so full of people with large packages, checked plastic bags the size of crates, two-seater passengers drawn from all parts of the globe, with arms full of stuff and stories.

A man with a crinkled face, the colour of seasoned oak, moves his legs to allow her to sit by the window.

"Had a good evening, love?"

"Yeah, very! How about you?"

He beams. "I've had a lovely time. Been in Deptford with my X. Spent the whole afternoon and evening with my old Mrs. Don't see her often . . . and my beautiful daughter, twenty-five . . . just graduated . . . I couldn't help myself. Embarrassed her, I did. Got her face between my hands and told her, told her I loved her to bits and how proud I was."

The creases round his eyes fan out to join the ripples surrounding his smile. He presses the bell.

"Hey love, this is me. See you around!"

Armageddon

Sue Ajax-Lewis

He awoke suddenly when the ground trembled under his feet and the vibrations began again. Panic-stricken, he ran down a tunnel with his community who had likewise been savagely woken.

It was the wrong direction. He turned and fled back the way he had come, panicking to get away as the dreadful noises and earth shaking under his feet confused him.

He was jostled by others seeking safety and not knowing where to find it. His feet scrabbled for stability as a tremor like an earthquake moved the ground underneath him. There was no light in the tunnels, just the awful darkness and the deafening pandemonium.

There was a solid thunderous crash and without warning the tunnel ahead collapsed, blocking his way. Many of his community died in front of him.

But through the collapsed tunnel, he spied daylight and ran towards it just before it was taken away from him, as more of the tunnel ahead broke down.

Once more, he turned and fled the other way.

Real panic now. No escape. Everywhere he ran, earthquakes under his feet and the dreadful vibrations confusing him, the cacophony of thunderous crashings and the darkness of the collapsing tunnels that the communities had made so long ago, before the terrifying destruction began, their peaceful harmonious and industrious lifestyle ripped from them.

He was only young and frightened and alone and jostled by others who ran past him in panic, terrified by the sudden onset of destruction and destitution of their world.

Blindly he followed them, relying on them to know what to do, where to go and how to get out of this terrible torment and somehow back to the peaceful, quiet existence they had always known. Surely they must know. Surely they would help him and show him the way.

He was panting now, running out of energy and willpower to go on.

Ahead, another exit collapsed and as one, the scurrying hordes ran back and he got jostled and trodden on and shoved aside as they fled past. Gamely, he turned around and tried to follow them as fast as he could.

There was another earth-quaking tremor but suddenly, ahead, light and air. Panting, he struggled towards it, fear giving him the adrenaline to fight to survive.

He pushed his head out of the ground. He gazed around in fresh terror. Where was all the grass and the greenness, the trees and the flowers?

He cried then. Crying for his mother, for the life that he had had and would never have again. Crying because he was so frightened and didn't know what to do and there was no one to ask.

Gulping in the dust-laden air, he raised his head to see if the sky was still the same.

But he couldn't see it.

What he did see was a huge digger-load of earth poised above his head, just before it was dumped on top of him. And the ant died.

Something to Celebrate

Audrey Lee

Many and many a year ago and a mystery or two away from here, Raven and Crow were having a game of chess. They were not exactly on the Night's Plutonian Shore but somewhere uncomfortably near to it, for both of them were very, very old indeed. Their feathers were thinning and their faculties diminishing. The game, perforce, was a simple one, as was their philosophy. You would think the years would have at least given them some wisdom, but that does not necessarily follow.

As you probably know, Crow is a lugubrious fellow at the best of times and Raven, also, has a problem promoting an atmosphere of cheerfulness. Inevitably, the game became heavy, the atmosphere dark, and between moves there was much sighing and bewailing the exigencies of life.

Raven moved White Pawn to E4 and sighed deeply. "You realise, Crow," he said, "Neither of us is more powerful than these chess pieces. Neither of us can step outside the rules of the game we play."

"Ah, indeed," groaned Crow, as he slowly moved Black Pawn to F5. "We are all – pieces and players – prisoners of pre-determined moves, whether the game be chess or life. Which of us can choose our fate?"

Now, a small white pawn overheard this and became very uneasy. It called out to the other pawns, "Is this true?"

"Oh, do not listen to Crow," answered several of them. "Crow is a pessimist. His eyes are as black as gun barrels. He will tell you chess is a game of war and we are the infantry."

"And perhaps we are!" piped up all the other pawns. "If only we could afford to stop and think about it! But we cannot risk moving backwards, we must always move on. Our survival depends on it!"

The pawns all started jumping up and down, "We can only be valuable and powerful if we survive! We must survive!" Several of them developed violent indigestion and had to stop.

The small white pawn grew more disturbed. Like so many of

71

his colleagues, he dreaded being captured and consigned to the further reaches of the Plutonian Shore, where all the prisoners were rested and then redeployed. It had dampened his enthusiasm for the game. "If Raven and Crow are right, why should we bother to go on? What is there to be cheerful about? Can we not even hope?"

"No hope, no hope at all," grumbled Crow, his voice like thunder in the distance. "Nothing to celebrate. Only war and death and struggle and famine."

"Can we return to the beginning?" enquired the pawn.

"Nevermore," roared Raven in a typically stentorian way, and moved White Pawn to F4.

There was a sudden wind and a knight appeared, his horse's hooves pounding the ground restlessly. "Have no fear! You can depend on me to have a really good idea. I am always courageous! I am waiting to fork and leap! I am a knight!" (There were cries of "Privilege! Privilege!" from the pawns). "I will find something to celebrate . . ." he said, and finding nowhere to fork or leap he cantered off.

"Can we not celebrate a win?" enquired Crow.

"No," said Raven. "A winner means a loser. We need more than that." And he wondered why he carried on with the game.

"Don't ask me to find a cause for celebration," uttered a plaintive small voice. It was the black king, standing alone and aloof. "I am a king but my power is all in my name. I can hardly move at all." He adjusted his crown, which had slipped, and cast a furtive sideways glance up at Crow. "Do your best, but I believe they are all out to get me. I am secretly afraid."

"Do not be afraid," said Crow. "If I get rid of the queen and the bishops and the knights and the rooks you will become powerful." He moved Black Pawn to G5, which was not a helpful thing to do.

Stalemate. Paralysis!

The bishop began to preach, but he had nothing to be pleased about, nothing to celebrate at all. The sly and wily bishop was itching to move diagonally, whichever way suited him, but he did not know which way to choose.

"Who would be a rook?" muttered a humble little voice. "We travel the pathway of suffering."

"You are my castle, my fore-square solid castle," said Raven. "Too bad you are forced to move in the shape of the cross. Nothing to celebrate there." He moved White Queen to H5.

Checkmate!

"The King is dead," pronounced Raven dramatically. "Long live the Queen!"

Suddenly every chess piece on the board began to jump up and down wildly. They had thought of something they could celebrate. The pawns, especially, were ecstatic. "We have only to reach the eighth rank of squares to become queens ourselves! Think of it!"

Then the white queen gathered her skirts, straightened her crown and drew herself up to her full height. She addressed the entire contingent of chess pieces in an aristocratic and motherly fashion.

"I am the Queen. I move in all directions. I am the most powerful piece on the board."

"Hurrah!" yelled the pawns.

"Hurrah!" cried all the other pieces.

"Because I am a woman, I can bend, retract, expand. I am multi-faceted. I can multi-task. I am mother and monarch."

"Hurrah for the Queen!" The shout went up on all sides. Here was truly something to celebrate. "Long live the Queen!"

"There appears to be a commotion among the chess pieces," said Raven, brightening up a little. He cupped his hand behind his ear. "Indeed! Perhaps a schism for the bishop to pontificate about? Perhaps a mutiny in the ranks of the pawns?"

"It sounds more like a celebration!" exclaimed Crow, who had better hearing.

"What is there to celebrate?" moaned Raven, resuming his former gloom.

"Your win?" enquired Crow, generously reminding him.

"Ah! Where is the glory in that? Win or lose, peace or war, it is all out of our hands. We are all pawns! Pawns, dear sir, all pawns in the hands of fate!"

Crow cawed dismally.

"Oh, shut up you sillies!" said a voice like a cello. "What do you know about it?"

"I beg your pardon!" said Crow, most offended. "Who is calling us sillies?"

"Yes! Who dares do that?" thundered Raven.

"It is I," said the Queen. "I, the most powerful piece on the board, who calls you sillies."

"Why?" queried both highly insulted parties.

"Because, although we may not choose our fate, or step outside the rules . . ."

"No need to rub it in," moaned Raven.

73

"Yes, no need to elaborate," groaned Crow.

"Just consider this," said the Queen. "Within the first four moves of the game, the number of possible manoeuvres you may consider come to some forty thousand. That enough for you Raven? That enough for you, Crow?"

"That's if we can think of them," said Crow.

"Another matter entirely," said the Queen.

After some time of reflection, and quiet murmuring of "Indeed!" and "Forty thousand!", Raven decided that on this occasion he might forego his nightly habit of croaking, "Nevermore!" He and Crow began to feel unusually lighthearted, and decided there would be no harm in joining in with the increasingly abandoned cries of acclaim for the wise and authoritative and altogether essential Queen.

Spirits of the Freeze-Sea

Suzanne Conboy Hill

All the Birthdays

When it's our birthday, when the ice breaks and the spirits burst through, you have to dodge out of the way and cover your head so they don't hiss sharp into your ears or quick-grab your tongue. If they get your tongue, you end up babbling like a prattaloon for days and people laugh and throw things at you to shut you up. Dilip got a broken nose that way last year, when a shelly-pot hit him. If they get in your ears, you're stuck listening to the flap-mouthing the babblers made all the years before, and that's worse because you can't shut them up and the spirits can be a bit choosy about how long they leave you with the racket. But you have to keep your eyes wide open because they want you to watch them while they dance and dive and scorch the air and cut sizzling streaks into the ice. You can blink, just so long as you don't linger. Blinking is okay.

Izzy got caught last year, twirling on the edge of the freeze-sea like a dizzy firefly with her head back and her arms wide, all shut-eyed and giddy. Burned her eyelids right off her face, they did. She'll be watching the rest of her life now, which won't be too much longer because Izzy has to share everyone's birthday so she gets everyone's years too, and there are near a hundred of us and nobody lives that long.

Dancing to the Wild Ice

After Izzy's eyelids got burned off, she had to watch all the time without blinking – apart from the frog-lick that slides across side-to-side, but you can see through that so there's no escape and she's been watching since Jinty started making the dance.

Izzy and Jinty and me are on the same birth ring – at least for now. When the ice breaks on your birthdays, you don't want to get distracted by the noises and the flap-yappering of the spirits getting into people's mouths and ears. If you do, you might forget to keep looking, like Izzy did. She won't be on our birth ring after the dance.

Making a dance is tricky; you can't just put it together from nothing with your own leggy-hops and chinbobs and such; there's a right way to do it. For a start, you have to make sure there's the same number of steps as celebrators. You can have multiples or squares or roots, but you can't have primes, they're sneaky and unfriendly, so you put harmonics on primes to layer them up, like chords for feet.

Jinty got permission to open the Book of Dances and stuffed leaves in his ears so the whistling wouldn't get into his head while he traced over the old patterns with blackwood chalk. Jinty plays cat-string harp and he knows harmonies but he's not good at numbers, so we blew the good ones into his left ear and the bad ones into his right ear and made marks on the backs of his hands so he'd remember.

He was gone half the year doing that dance with only the tapping and thumping to say he was still in the Book House. We pushed bits of bovey meat and pea parkies under the door to keep him going, and we tried not to sing in case we put him off his rhythm and he got something wrong. The problem with being the dance-maker is that, if you got it wrong, you have to join the dancer and do the dance together, hopping over the ice from beat to beat and picking up more and more birthdays on the way. Of course, it means you share them with the dancer so you only pick up half each, which can be a blessing, as long as it doesn't leave you with the head-dallies and not being able to think straight. Then you'll straightaway make a mistake and end up stiff as a snowfish with your eyeballs pointing at the sky and the deep at the same time.

Jinty's doing it because he got the green twig and there's a lot of us on our ring so not much chance of coming back if he fouls up. Not like when there's only, say, ten or twenty of you. You can add ten or twenty birthdays no problem as long as you don't already have a whole lot stacked up. There's over two hundred of us, and we have twenty five rings, and nobody lives that long.

We knew he was done when the spirits started chasing about above the Book House, whipping the roofing up at the corners and screeching through the windows like banshee-ghosts riding on lightning. It was going to be our birthdays tomorrow so there wasn't any more time. Anyway, he came out, pulling the dance along behind him on wax-leaf runners and it twitched and throbbed like it was ready to go all on its own. We all helped to pin it down – spitting on its edges and freezing it to the ice. The last step had to be in the right place for Izzy, in the middle where the wild ice shifted and sucked like a whirlpool full of skinning knives. We could see the spirits under the surface, charging about with trails of fire behind them, and we made sure to keep looking. Izzy was looking too, of course, but even with the doze-weed it was like she knew this was for her. She'd be stepping and hopping and gathering years to her back until she was stooped, but if Jinty had got it right and we'd done the freezing out right, Izzy would drop into the wild ice just before her skin fell off and her arms and cheeks and bones came apart, and her blood and water and gristle spread over the lake to feed the shinny beetles. It wouldn't be so bad if she couldn't feel any of it. It wouldn't be so bad if the rest of us couldn't hear any of it either, but we only had the doze-weed. Jinty'd had no doze-weed and he was scrabbit-scared. We'd know tomorrow if he had good reason.

Shalla's First Ice Shatter

There was a whole lot of whooping and clapping and shrieking coming from the Meeting House yesterday. Bunches of ten year olds skipping up the steps in their fancy drapes, and bunches of little ones prancing about outside like dolly-mops on strings, pretending to be grown-ups with flaps on their ears and their mouths lip-tight shut.

When each batch got inside the house, with the big doors closed and their child years shut off for good, the instructing began for their first Ring Birthdays. You have to know how to stop the yollerers getting into your head, and how to always watch the ice spirits, to keep looking and never to close your eyes except to blink.

It's Shalla's year this time and she's all excited and looking forward to her first ice shatter, seeing the spirits shooting like hiss-rockets out of the freeze-sea to rip up the sky and make witchcats out of the clouds. She's never seen a witchcat – well, you don't until your first birthday because of the risk you might forget to look where you should look, and you end up having your own dance made for you. When that happens, they give you doze-weed to get you through it, but you still collect everyone else's birthdays and get older and older as you go. You might be lucky and draw a good dance maker; get to the end before the end gets to you.

After the hi-jinks and sweetpops and little pieces of stripy rock-gum, it all went quiet and the humming began. You hum because it helps the words settle in, like humming makes a soft place in your head for them to sink into and stick. But with over a hundred first timers, there's bound to be a few accidents. You just hope you've done enough and there weren't any nippers in the air, stealing the words out of the little ones' ears and leaving scrabflannels in their place.

There's shrieking in the Meeting House again today because they're strapping Shalla into the gripframe. After her sister forgot to keep looking at the spirits and ended up dancing over the sea-ice with her bones on fire, Shalla's parents aren't taking any chances. Stretching her eyelids over the frame and finishing them off there and then, she won't have to be stitched wide open every year. There won't be the holes and the darn-beds; the bits of gut weft, greased out stiff like they're pretending to be eyelashes. And with a good sharp slick-knife, those eyelids will come off easy as a lizard skin.

Western Fantasy

Jackie Harvey

Bob stretched his rotund figure full length on the sofa, a half-eaten pizza beside him next to a bottle of lager. He burped. The television was emitting the usual noisy adverts, interrupting his favourite game show. What to watch now? He went through the Netflix menu but he'd watched it all. The well-worn remote control sat firmly in his warm hand. He gave out a bored yawn, pressing the button for "Westerns 1950's". Well, that might be entertaining, despite being in black and white. He'd not seen one of those films for years.

The title flashed on the screen: "The Lone Ranger". Cowboys and Indians raced each other across the desert plains, whilst raucous music blared. Bob laughed, how old-fashioned it seemed. Just make believe, surely life could never have been like that? But he was intrigued and captivated. It made a change from the blood and violence of the films he usually liked to watch, and it was action packed.

He took another gulp of his lager and rearranged himself on the sofa until comfy. His eyelids grew heavy and he began to doze.

Dazzling lights bounded around his head, whilst his body elevated itself into a spinning spiral. Bob felt the suction as his body headed for the TV screen. He waited for the crunch and splintering of glass. But there was none.

The sounds of gunfire, shouting and thundering of hooves enveloped him. Sunshine and desert scenery greeted his eyes. As far as he could see, giant cacti, shrub and sand filled his vision. Where am I? Something shot past him and landed at his feet. An arrow. But where from? He turned to face the dazzling sunshine. A dozen half-clad Indians on their painted ponies galloped towards him, feathered headdresses waving in the wind. Bob froze. There was no way out, nowhere to run.

"What do you want?" He stood rigid but his legs shook uncontrollably.

The Indians came to an abrupt halt a short distance from him, quietly staring. The face-painted chief approached him menacingly, gesturing with his bow for Bob to move closer. A sudden shout emitted from one of the Indians and they all turned. Amidst a cloud of dust, a white horse appeared, nostrils blazing. Astride him sat a masked figure, his gun aimed towards the Indians. He fired a bullet, hitting one close to him who fell to the ground. The others scattered, shouting and screaming.

The white horse reared. "Hi ho, Silver!" shouted the masked rider.

Bob stood frozen. Could it be, surely not, the real Lone Ranger? This was too much. He'd had enough. After all, it was a dream wasn't it? He must wake up; anyway, he needed another lager.

From inside the TV, he pressed hard against the screen, but there was no give. It was solid and firm. He hit the screen again. Nothing.

"Help, get me out of here!" His scream went unheard. There was no one there.

My Wobbly Table

Michael Wearing

Bill had seen the table on display in the charity shop. It looked perfect, exactly what he needed. Bill found it entertaining and fulfilling to write letters to newspapers and politicians. His letters were more often than not pedantic ramblings. Politicians usually replied with a simple "thank you for your letter, I will look into it and get back to you in due course". To Bill, it appeared that due course never actually came and that's predominately because it didn't. He'd even written a letter complaining about this to his MP and got a letter back which he had framed and hung on his wall. "Thank you for your letter concerning the letters written to me to which you haven't received replies. I will look into the issue and get back to you in due course." Editors of newspapers, on the other hand, never replied to Bill. It didn't dampen his spirit. He kept on writing to them.

Bill, with dyed black hair and bushy eyebrows that put a squirrel's tail to shame, was very much a loner. He had always typed his letters on a laptop rested on his lap. He assumed that's what you did; after all why else call it a laptop? It was only when he was repairing the hole in his shed roof (which had been caused when the National Anthem came on the radio and he had stood to attention and pretended to present arms with a hoe in his hands) that he noticed his neighbour working at a table on a laptop that it dawned on him that he needed a table.

Bill was now sitting at the table, but there was a problem: the table wobbled. Bill got on his hands and knees and examined the table legs. Three legs were touching the ground but one wasn't. When he pulled that leg down to the ground the opposite leg went up. When he let go of the leg it resumed a position half an inch from the ground. He had purchased a wobbly table and there was nothing he could do to alter that.

Bill always attended the local boot fair, even though the organisers hadn't replied to his letter complaining about the fact that the stalls should be clustered together according to what they were selling. He had explained that he wasn't interested in children's toys, but he had to walk past many stalls selling them. If they were clustered together he could avoid them entirely. He could go to the area that sold exactly what he had come to the boot fair for.

Of course, Bill didn't ever know what he was looking for. Subconsciously, he was looking for something to write a letter of complaint about, but consciously he hadn't a clue. He was there on a summer morning when he spotted a stall selling an array of what antique dealers call junk. He wondered what sort of household could possibly have owned a teapot styled as a cottage, rusty garden shears, a plastic bonsai tree and a six-foot-long wooden snake. He was trying to compose a suitable question in his head when he noticed a book under the leg of the pasting table that was acting as the stall. Bill carefully removed the book, passed 50p to the middle-aged stall holder, who was happy to pocket it despite now having an unstable table.

Bill cut short his visit to the boot fair and rushed home. Pleased with his purchase, he smiled as he looked at it, before kneeling down by his table and placing the book under the short leg. The book was too thin, the table leg didn't reach it and consequently the table still wobbled. Bill pondered a while then removed the book. He tried placing it under the other way up. That of course made no difference.

Bill was confused. He thought he had a solution to his wobbly table, but all that had happened was that he was now angry that he had wasted his money. He was about to bin the book when he noticed the title: *How to Write and Be Published*. He glanced inside the book, and before realising what he was doing he was sitting reading the book.

As soon as he had finished the last sentence, he opened up his laptop, and started to type in bold capital letters: "MY WOBBLY TABLE". He then continued to type. Nobody ever visited Bill, so no one saw him typing word after word, day after day, week after week, month after month. Consequently, nobody saw Bill when the day finally arrived when he typed the words THE END. He was pleased with himself. It had taken months for him to complete. He had not written a letter to anyone whilst writing his book, not the council, not the local newspaper, nor his MP. He had been totally focused on completing *My Wobbly Table*. Now, all he had to do was fill in a few boxes as required by the publisher's website, attach a PDF file of the book, and they would do the rest. This time he knew his writing would be published because he was self-publishing.

Bill checked his door each time the postman came. The only mail he received were a few circulars, a gas bill and a letter addressed to his next-door neighbour that was accidentally delivered to the wrong address. Rather than popping it through his neighbour's letterbox , Bill wrote "Delivered to the wrong address" on the envelope and walked the 400 yards to post in the nearest postbox.

When the parcel finally arrived, he excitedly grabbed it from the postman, ripping it open to reveal his book. *My Wobbly Table* by Bill Hartson had arrived. He stared at the cover for about a minute before bending down and placing it under the shorter of the table legs. It was a perfect fit. The table would wobble no more.

More Things in Heaven and Earth

Norman Allcorn

There are more things in Heaven and Earth than are dreamed of in your philosophy, so Hamlet tells Horatio in Will Shakespeare's play.

Philosophy was the last thing on the mind of the Allcorn family when they moved to Priory Farm in 1943. They were more concerned as to how to manage without any "mod cons". The toilet was a bucket, the water from a well, and lighting by oil lamp or candles, but then that was how people had lived for many, many years.

As its name suggests, the farmhouse was built from the ruins of a former priory. An order of Augustinian Black Canons had established a priory at Hastings sometime in the 12th century. By 1406, it was threatened by the sea. Sir John Pelham gave land for a new one, deep in the woods at Warbleton, in East Sussex, and it became active in 1413. Records show that it was not run in a very circumspect way, and it was abolished, like so many others, by Henry VIII in 1536. It fell into decay and in the 17th century an ironmaster's house was built using stone from the former chapel. This became a farmhouse on the demise of the iron industry.

Locals told how the house was haunted by the ghosts of two monks who had killed each other over a girl. There was a red patch (a bloodstain?) on a floorboard in the front bedroom This did not fit the timespan, but why ruin a good story over a couple of hundred years! One earlier tenant, who took paying guests, put down some red paint every year so as not to disappoint his visitors. Another story tells of a ghostly monk, who on Christmas Eve rises up out of the pond at the entrance to the farm.

There were two skulls at the house in the 19th century, and it was said that they were of these same two monks. If they were removed from the house, there was a triple curse:

1. Should a stranger look at them there would be a terrific storm.
2. Should anyone touch them, they would pass through the valley of the shadow of death.
3. Should they be removed from the Priory, the crops would fail and the cattle get ill.

By 1906, the skulls had gone from the Priory but were causing trouble to whoever had them, with strange noises in the night.

There is one field at the Priory called Redlands, on account of its colour caused by high iron content. One earlier farmer found that he could not keep cattle in this field, but sheep thrived in it. Was this part of the curse or just a natural phenomenon?

There were no skulls there in 1943 and the farm was productive apart from one incident. The bullocks were infested with warble flies. These insects lay eggs on the legs of cattle which hatch into larvae who migrate through the body and come out through lumps on the back. The treatment at this time was pyrethrum powder, but this was unobtainable in war time, so a nicotine solution was used. This got into the bloodstream and the bullocks were very ill, although none died. (Systemic insecticides have eradicated warble flies since 1990.)

The Allcorns were sensible farming people and dismissed all this ghost talk as nonsense. True, there were many strange noises in this old draughty farmhouse. Little owls nesting in the roof made scuttling noises on the ceiling. There were also bats who got behind the wallpaper with much fluttering. The paper was on canvas stretched over beams. A candle was seen in an empty room but that was moonlight shining off a twisted diamond pane. So they made fun of it, and almost took it too lightly.

Mrs Allcorn's father was visiting and she slid back the foot-square opening in the door to the sitting room, then screamed and rattled an old chain. He almost had a heart attack.

Old pictures of the house show a very tall chimney over the kitchen. This was unsafe and was rebuilt, but the builders could see no reason to go so high and it was lowered. Afterwards it smoked if the wind was in the east! This also gave rise to another unexpected happening. Mrs Allcorn had an artist friend to stay, with her small daughter and husband, another artist. He wanted a separate bedroom as his daughter was keeping him awake. In the middle of the night, he rushed to his wife's room saying, "There really are ghosts here." In the morning, a piece of mortar was discovered in the fireplace of his bedroom. It had fallen down from the previous repair.

In 1962, the skulls resurfaced. They were found in a biscuit tin, in the cellar of an antiques dealer in the lanes in Brighton. After checking that they really were old, they were returned to the Priory. Mrs Vi Allcorn was dubious about having them but Mr Jack Allcorn was unmoved. One skull had the top missing, as if sliced off with a sharp blade. The other was more complete, with a jaw bone. This one he would hold like a ventriloquist's dummy and say, "Look, he is smiling." Vi was not amused but Jack was unrepentant. That is, until he had three accidents in quick succession (what was that about the valley of the shadow of death?):

1. A barn door blew shut during a gale and injured his shoulder.
2. Just as he was walking past a stack of bales, some wet ones fell on him.
3. He was driving a new tractor when the steering broke and he drove down a six foot bank into Christian's River. This was not quite as bad as it sounds, as the river was in fact just a small stream.

Nothing more happened, so was the curse satisfied?

When the Allcorns left the farm, Jack hid the skulls in the loft. They were found some years later when the Priory was turned into a hotel. The owner then appeared in the local paper to promote the hotel. He had one skull in each outstretched hand! The Priory was a hotel for several years until it failed and he is no longer the owner! It is now a private house. Let us hope that the present occupants respect the skulls and that they listen to Hamlet's words.

There are more things in Heaven and Earth, Horatio, than are dreamed of in your philosophy.

The Custom of April Fool's Day, April 1st

Alan Lawrie

One form of humour is the prank and prankster.

Virtually every country in the world devises a harmless, practical joke on April 1st in a jovial way (an adjective for Jupiter or Zeus, King of the Gods on Mount Olympus renowned for his sense of mirth, joy and laughter – one thinks of the actor Brian Blessed making an excellent Zeus).

The idea is to fool you but it often has a reverse effect where fooled people take it all literally.

Jovian–Plutonian gravitational effect: In 1976, British astronomer Sir Patrick Moore told listeners of BBC Radio 2 that unique alignment of two planets would result in an upward gravitational pull making people lighter at precisely 9:47 am that day. He invited his audience to jump in the air and experience "a strange floating sensation.

Dozens of listeners phoned in to say the experiment had worked, among them a woman who reported that she and her 11 friends were "wafted from their chairs and orbited gently around the room."

It is generally agreed that greatest hoax ever was "The Saghetti Tree Harvest". On April 1, 1957, the BBC broadcast a film in their *Panorama* current affairs series purporting to show Swiss farmers picking freshly-grown spaghetti, in what they called the Swiss Spaghetti Harvest. The segment said the harvest enjoyed a "bumper year" thanks to mild weather and the elimination of the spaghetti weevil.

Many credulous Britons were taken in, and why not? The story was on television – then a relatively new invention – and Auntie Beeb would never lie, would she?

The BBC were soon flooded with requests to purchase a spaghetti plant, forcing them to declare the film a hoax on the news the next day.

If you google "BBC Spaghetti-Harvest in Ticino" on YouTube you will see for yourself how this 3-minute cleverly constructed footage fooled everyone.

The story was ranked the No. 1 April Fools' hoax of all time by the Museum of Hoaxes website – a fine source for all things foolish. But the BBC with its voice of authority, perfect English and deadpan delivery would not be allowed to pull a stunt like this today.

No one seems to be sure how all this originated but in 1686, a certain John Aubrey referred to April 1st as "Fooles Holy Day" (which, incidentally, is where we get the word Holi-day) as the first British reference to it. On April 1, 1698, several people were tricked into going to the Tower of London to see the Lions washed.

This wonderful tradition survives because it gives us all lighthearted relief from daily stress.

The Taco Liberty Bell was an April Fool's Day joke played by fastfood restaurant chain Taco Bell. The ad was created by Jon Parkinson and Harvey Hoffenberg who worked at Bozell, the Taco Bell advertising agency at the time.

In this now-classic 1996 prank, Taco Bell took out newspaper ads saying it had bought the Liberty Bell "in an effort to help the national debt."

Even some senators were taken in, and the National Park Service held a press conference to deny the news.

At noon, the fastfood chain admitted the joke and said it was donating $50,000 for the landmark bell's care.

Thousands of people had called Taco Bell headquarters and the National Park Service before it was revealed at noon on April 1 that the story was a hoax.

The value of the joke, of course, was priceless.

PART TWO

POETRY

A Leaf

Caroline Collingridge

What are you, leaf? I ask in my grief.
I found you on the forest floor and, what's more
I found you in the book I'm reading.
You're everywhere, but I'm still bleeding.

You're scrumpled up, crushed under foot
But oh so green, just sprouted from the twig.
Soft and velvety, yet ridged with spines
Carrying food to the furthest vines.

Can I take a leaf from your stem?
Can I learn what it is you impart?
Do you have a page I can read?
Or a book I can keep to treat as a seed?

Leaf so thin yet full of soul
You carry the whole tree within you
You're flat, your blades are your land
Leaf hand, tree stand, fern band.

Follow the lines, don't drop from the tree,
Not yet, until I've seen you grow green,
Turn yellow, orange, gold and red,
Your skeleton finally laid to bed.

Then you show me your life,
I'm in the palm of your hand.
I'll have a love petal in my heart
I'll have the leaf from which to start.

Memento

Cherrie Taylor

It used to be on the wall by my bed…
No I don't keep it hidden. I didn't expect you to pry.
You don't understand I loved him.
Don't look at me like that – we all loved him
it wasn't just me. No one talks about his good side.
He was kind. There were others – they were to blame.
Give the book to me. Go! Leave, if you can't hear
what I say – what I remember. I was there after all.
I wanted to marry him. I know he was older
a lot older… but it was my dream.
I talked about it with my parents.
They understood, even though they laughed.
"Our little Ema wants to marry a god!"
I understood much later and of course…
it would have ended in tears. It all ended in tears…
No, he never visited. He never came to our home.
He would have been so welcomed if he had –
he would have loved our dog. She was a pure-bred
like *Blondi.* He would have stroked her and ruffled her coat
like he ruffled my hair. He bent down and took my face
in his hands. His eyes were a beautiful blue – so clear.
Piercing? No, not the eyes I saw. The eyes that smiled
at me – they were honest – big blue eyes like stars.
They were tearful too. I think he knew I loved him.
I was just a child watching him pass by.
My heart leapt with love.
The swastika? Oh that's a keepsake too.

Field Place Afterwards

Lawrence Long

(Written after a WSW Day For Writers there)

Silence has fallen back on the bowling lawns
Bubble, ferment of creative brains gone away
Mindset running through the cerebella
You have put to bed another day

The beauty of the word is back in covers
The thought processes they took from this grass
Will be the fountainhead of future fiction
Let it come, let it be, let it pass

We have brought the beauty of the language
Brought things that did not exist before
Ours is not the only group or language
But it is what we share by the shore

You brought the day and organisation
We brought work and brains and hearts
The tutors brought ideas and inspiration
We cared, we shared, and now the day departs

But the day departs in a blaze of sunshine
White flannels, long shadows on the lawn
We have taken, we have drunk real fine
Of sweet nectar that will lead us on.

Just Friends

Norman Allcorn

What might have been with you and me,
What could have been our destiny,
If we had met when both were free.
Many many years ago.

Could we still know a youthful thrill,
And have we 'got it' still,
Or are we now 'over the hill',
Here in the present day.

We meet and talk and yet I still
Do not know the way you feel
About me. Is it real
Or just a dream.

We now are bound by our life past,
We've vows to keep that have to last,
And so *just friends*; the die is cast.
But, perhaps not forever.

Who knows what the future has in store,
Or what stories are there, yet; galore,
When the wheel of fortune turns once more,
And the arrow points to – us

Or is it all now far too late,
The sands of time they just won't wait,
And so is this to be our fate,
Forever, *Just Friends*.

Solitude

Caroline Collingridge

A buttercup, alone in the field, faces the sun,
Warmed, enlightened.
A butterfly flitters in the wind,
Lands on a foxglove and finds nectar.

Whistling in the trees, then it's gone,
Shooshing, whooshing, haaaa...
A swift screeches – aah eee aah eee –
It has found its nest at last.

Sitting by a tree feeling its roots,
Gurgling, gushing with food.
Soft moss, so velvet, cushions me.
Lichen, the treasures of the forest.

Silence at last, peace beyond.
Senses so full, now at rest.
Safety in aloneness
   glow
   waft
   sink
   soul
   be

Therapy Room

Fran Tristram

through frosted glass
light falls
on an empty vessel

exquisitely crafted, it is made
from a material so soft
that it is as insubstantial
to the touch as air
on a balmy day

from a material so hard
that a wildly swinging demolition ball
leaves not so much
as a scratch

a material so bright
that it perfectly reflects
everything
that we bring to it

so resonant
that it echoes even that
which we hardly dared
to whisper

a material so yielding and elastic
that there is always space
to accommodate
a little more

Seeds

Theresa Gooda

Genesis.
In late winter I sowed so many seeds,
spending time in a blindly hopeful gamble:
covered them in dirt knowing nothing
would appear at all for weeks, if ever.
Petulant frost did for some, one starred night
when the greenhouse door was left wide open;
heat did for more when scorching sun crippled
through radiating glass that should protect.

Exodus.
In April, I planted out, after what
I'd heard was the last of the cold. It wasn't.
Demeter's grief had miles further to run,
adding to my hurt. Nodding bedding plants,
begonia and petunia, lost their heads.
Little red mouths stopped smiling. Frozen
corpses lay in that cold bed, unblanketed.

Leviticus.
My daughter, high priestess of Pinterest
taste, helped with re-planting. She wore
my gloves, hands nearly my size,
I had to show her how to break hardground.
I watched her choose new places, pattern earth.
So more of that blasted blind hope returns,
with Persephone, broadcast to the winds.

Tides

Theresa Gooda

It looks like a pork scratching or cracked bat wing. Maybe
a beetle body turned upside down, skeletal debris
from a scalding cauldron, dusk-discarded.
With the toe of my boot I dislodge the empty husk. Hard

to believe this brittle embryo-carcass was once fluid, sea-soft.
A membraned, pulsing capsule of some wave-tossed
creature and her kin, delicate tentacles curtseyed
to Neptune with treasure packed inside a mermaid

purse. And I remember the surly teenager
with her sand-fin tail, who walked old summers here.
Now, autumn rain pinches cold across the beach.
I shiver inside my hood, flinch at the seagull's screech.

Broken Stone

Rose Bray

I search for a flicker of life,
lift heavy slabs with bare hands,
in frenzy mine the rubble deeper
with strength I didn't know I had.

I see the baby fingers.
Still. Cold. Splayed in perfect form.
The tiny coat I made last year.
The face and hair are rimed with grit,
he looks asleep, my little one.

Just seven moons my son has lived.
I rock and rock his lifeless form.
Through my body tremors move,
strange, low sounds – an animal in pain.
I hear a keening, is it mine?

My first-born cries in terror,
arms outstretched she comes to me.
"Not yet!" I cry, pushing her away
shielding myself against the need to care,
for my heart is broken stone.

Cracked, twisted, the water pipe stands.
Unchecked, it ebbs its life away,
oozing, staining, ochre rubble.
Buried deep, chatter, laughter
last night it was my home.

I wet my veil to wash his face
stroke dust from thick, dark lashes,
imprint his image on my mind.
At sunset when earth holds its breath,
gentle hands will prise him from me.

I Want the World to Know

Michael Wearing

Exactly which way to go,
I don't want to fight in wars,
However good the cause.
Bombs scare me.
Hear my plea!
End this madness.
Stop this sadness.
I've got love to give,
So let me live.
Decide not what I should do.
Politicians, who are you?
You the law makers,
You the life takers.
You're all so intent on power,
Climbing up the highest tower.
Stepping on your friends,
To obtain your ends.
You'll never ever walk tall,
If you destroy us all.

If not today...

Paul Doran

The tanks are not far away
the sky is alight and we smell and see smoke
it's not safe to go out
rockets, shells keep us awake
the children scream and cry, they're hungry, so are we
they don't understand, I can't explain
my family and good friends are in Russia, scared,
they can't believe what's happening.

We're now packed in, under ground
we could try to leave the country, you can't
and you are risking your life for us, for our country
we hear of friends and neighbours killed defending us.

The children need me
I need you, I love you
I don't want to hear the news again
I want it all to stop
I want to be me again
my eyes are red, I'm weak with fear,
for the children, for you, for myself
my heart is dying.

Please, please come back soon, marry me.

A Moment in Time

Mary Jones

When High Kings robe
and mortals tremble,
and blackened hags of night ride at your elbow,
caper at your feet,
bring cadaverous invitation to macabre desire.
White violets, marsh grown, plead
no morning here.

No dawning here.
Dark invitations of imagination,
screen Archetypes of devastation.
heaping on us desolation
with increasing immolation,
dissolving into fragmentation,
Volcanic Ash.
Purple saxifrage enraged, engorges understanding
Whirlpool dark in depth, expanding,
Makes equation
Of Annihilation.

Then comes the Other,
Silent laden, Wisdom takes her stand.
Sophia pours the purifier, calmly from her loving hand.
And once again, the gift is given,
Light restores hearts to natural rhythm.

Due Date

Anne Dryden

Will it be today we get to meet?
Will your eyes be blue? – My heart skip a beat?

Will my waters break in some inconvenient place?
In Tesco – before I have packed my case?

Will I give birth in the car, with a policeman present?
Will your father be late and miss your advent?

Entonox might be fun to inhale.
Will I be serene, or will I wail?

Will I have pethidine in my thigh?
Or scream "epidural" before night passes by?

Ventouse, forceps, episiotomy, tear.
An emergency section! How much will I bare?

You take shape on my belly. You elbow and kick,
as we lie on the sofa and watch the clock tick.

Learning to Dance in the Rain

Anne Callaghan

When the season changes the cold Mistral comes
Breaking windows, slamming doors and bowing trees forever
towards the South

The desert flowers sense the imminent Samoon but it enters
every orifice of the unsuspecting
then envelops the traveller like the crust of a baking Sambousek
as it reshapes the landscape shifting the dunes as if they were
dust

The rage of the black Bora builds up slowly then lasts for hours
sometimes days blasting over the Adriatic splintering ships and
crashing cargo against the rocks

The mischief making devils of the Willy Willy whirl across the
bush whipping the tinder straw into shape

Tropical cyclones meet in typhoon alley following a parabola
northward at the speed of flight mugging everyone in their path,
then the cloudbursts carry away spiralling cattle, bodies and
homes

And all the while we sit behind a crumbling wall and wait for
the gentle breeze of the warming Zephyr

One of Those Days

Liz Eastwood

"I fling a great pearl of grief with all my strength at the sea's Apathy" (Ted Walker, 1934-2004)

Let's say it's one of those undeniable days
the gate sketches sun stripes down sea lane
the latch burns my hand as I start on my way
to our café on the shore   looking for more found
objects   I collect four remarkable round stones
for your solo sculptures of sea horses sitting on rocks

And say the waves and sun draw on mystical rocks
then paint blue tinged displays on a once cloudy day
of blue winged silhouette gulls that intersect stones
between blue beach huts playing at houses by the lane
then pop black rockweed the summer tide has found
and light on little terns gleaning prey as is their way

at low tide   I carry my lacquered box which weighs
more than my Fair Trade organic tote bag full of rocks
then seek polished shingle jewels the sea has found
then I make a ring with red kelp knots to mark the day
a crimson linnet twits his melody in the spit by the lane
where spiral rack blows bubbles amongst the stones

Suppose you send me a text *café 10 mns got 4 stns?*
then I pick yellow horned poppies in a crazy way
add furry leaves of starry clover I found in the lane
tie my posy with string   left by fishers on the rocks
where sea horses ride the waves like snakes all day
then I collect all the beached starfish that can be found

Let's say I choose the five best jewels I've found
select five silken opium poppy flowers for five stones
fold one scarlet petal round each treasure in *my* way
salting them in rock pools   this way *they'll last for days*
I arrange gem parcels on the sandy beach by the rocks
and gently line my box with rockweed from the lane

I open my bag to find my linnet song from the lane
and cry for any God for my tune is lost not found
I fling a great pearl of grief   with all my strength at the sea's
apathy   I decide to sacrifice my gems on the rocks
but I can't throw them to the waves like any old stones
so I set them on the bed of rockweed in *my own* way
Let's just say it's one of those indecipherable days

Suppose you say I should throw those stones away
stop wasting days meandering up and down the lane
I try to say   over lattes   how much more I've found than rocks

Book Rape

Liz Eastwood

It was at the Literary Group that I lost my lover,
My Flesh and Blood Poems by C K Williams book.
Today she came back. Two pages missing and the stains
Of cigaretty fingers that de-flyed . . . no typo . . . penetration . . . inside
Her secret pre formed, profound, pre destined passages. It has
Bruises on the bottom of page two; no emotions on the Cover.

If this happens to you, you won't know how to recover
From the police reports that tell you your lover's
Abuser remains unfound. She cannot tell me where she has
Been or what or who has been through her. My book
Has two pages missing; she's not the same book. Inside
The back cover see twisted, toying digits' disgusting stains.

On page twenty – "The Mistress", "The Lover" – give us strains
Of "a bloody beast" and a "lying bastard", the next page I discover
Is now twenty three – "Failure" and "Crime" – eyes seek tears turned out inside.
I paid five pounds ninety five to become her lover.
She thought she'd be left on the shelf, just another book
For the spine show; but I covet under her cover – so she never has.

Perking *it* up's impossible, now he's prised and poked at private pages. Has
Any other . . . other . . . man . . . had his fingers inside? Are those stains
Sticky coffee, cigarettes, crack line and wine? Look book,
Tell the truth. Did you let him? All over your cover?
Is his bookmark bigger than mine? Is he your secret lover?
Scream, book, mime from that vile, verb of violation inside.

I should have held on to her, kept her hidden inside
With Plath and Ted, by "The Door" where daring Atwood has
Visions; I stuff bloody, honeyed squirrels at wake of sullied lover.
The worst is not the squirrel's guts or gory entrails. Fucking honey stains.
Sixteen years we've been together. I think of me, how I'll recover.
I'm so bloody selfish, I don't think of The Book.

I was so bloody selfish, I didn't think of The Book.
I didn't know where to turn since he'd been inside.
She opened herself at page thirty eight and hid back cover.
We took our fill of "Will" and "Pregnant", raw sound of wound has
Seen innocence off but, wisely, she opens wide pages to stains
Of "Peace" on page thirty nine begging me to still be her lover.

If you look carefully you'll see that The Book has
Let me back in spite of me. Her elegy, her energy is the breath of survivors' stains.
See "First Desires" on page six. Excuse me I'm off to cover my lover.

Like the Back of My Hand

John Rudkin

Who finds no path where the pathway should be?
Who walks with his eyes closed refusing to see?
Who finds he has fallen in that old trap
of ditching the compass and scrapping the map?
Who places his faith in some short cut, close by,
that never appears? Who then wonders why
he seems to be wandering some unknown track?
Blundering onward, too tired to turn back.
Who ignores signposts? Refuses to stay
to listen to natives who *do* know the way?
Says in his head that he knows the direction
so well, he can tell that it needs no correction.
Who's limping through life in *this* sort of mess?
I ask, "Is it me?" and my conscience cries, "Yes!"

The Coy Mistress Replies

Patricia Feinberg Stoner

(A response to Andrew Marvell's poem "To His Coy Mistress"*)*

Oh Andy, stop your mithering, do!
I really do not fancy you.
You praise my eyes, my cheek, my lips
I'd rather have some fish and chips.
You praise my brow, my neck, my nose,
But you don't give a fig for those.
Yet when it comes to snowy breasts
You would adore each, east and west,
And if I let you, you'd go south
But I deny your questing mouth.
It puts me in a blinding rage
When you say you'd take an age
To worship me – that's such a bore!
I don't think love should be a chore.
It makes my very blood run cold
When you speak of getting old.
And when you mention graves, I trow,
That's for tomorrow, not for now.
Don't think I'm not completely wise
To all your scheming, tricks and lies:
If present mirth has present laughter
I know *exactly* what you're after.
I know you want to bill and coo
But Coronation Street is due.
You want some sex? Well, not a hope:
I'd much prefer to watch my soap.
To summarise: you're out of luck
If you're looking for a bit of slap and tickle.

I Was Once

Audrey Lee

(a true story)

I was once a serious poet. I had flair! I had ambition!
I thought only angst and metaphor brought poets recognition.
I read Eliot at night. Man, he was a thinker, he was deep!
Eliot TS and George – they got me off to sleep.
I grappled with Ted Hughes and Plath, I studied form and meter
I embraced aesthetic irony – bought an electric heater.
I loved strange words like antistrophe and magic words like meta
synaesthesia and jouissance – ah, the more obscure the better.
I went to this class on James Joyce – devoured each turgid article
Now, he was a serious poet BUT*he married Nora Barnacle!!!*
I remember thinking – funny that – it's really rather farcical
I mean, you couldn't make it up, a name like Nora Barnacle.
"Nora Barnacle?" I cried, "I'd rather starve! Boom, Boom!"
and not a flicker of a smile travelled round that room.
In that class of intellectuals I might have known before I spoke
they were far too intellectual to recognise a joke.
It was then that I got fed up with Joyce and clever blokes like him
and decided to abandon them and write this sort of thing.

Maroon

Alex Medwell

Hard to see his face in your mind,
the army man dressed in maroon.
The only memory from such young age;
colour of red velvet macaroon.
He gave his life trying to save
other lives from a terrorist bomb.
Know how much he'd care and love,
if he hadn't been long gone.
He never meant to maroon you
as a child on his parents' farm.
Commitment to the Medical Corps
was never intended to cause you harm.
You never knew the date he died,
so grieve on each remembrance day.
It was during The Troubles, not World War One.
It's how you mourn, not when, anyway.
So spend all day remembering your dad.
Let this nor nothing else distract.
But good to know while you think of him,
someone is thinking of you – it's fact.
(P.S. He loves you)

PART THREE

BIOGRAPHIES

Sue Ajax-Lewis

SueAjax Lewis is a modestly published writer with aspirations to finishing her novel(haven't we all?).A flight attendant for nearly thirty years, she flew around the world and was fortunate enough to meet and work with some lovely people. Now gently retired,she loves being able to devote more time to writing and walking inthe woods with her dogs.She finds West Sussex Writers a hugely inspirational fellowship of support and advice and more lovely people.

Norman Allcorn

Norman Allcorn is a new member to WSW,although older than the club itself. Coming from a farming background, he spent many years milking cows and some with the local electricity board. During his long retirement, he has enjoyed gardening and showing his dogs, now alas all gone. His interest in archaeology, history, and family history started him writing, and during lockdown he wrote and published a book on the Allcorn family.

Terence Brand

Terence Brand joined theRoyal Air Force as a boy and served in the Middle and Far East. Onentering Civvy Street, he worked in electronics and communications andlater ran a retail business selling hi-fi. After an early retirement, hetook up writing, initially to keep the brain ticking over. He regularlyattends creative writing classes and joined West Sussex Writers in 1997.

Rose Bray

Rose Bray was born and grew up in the Isle of Man. She trained as a teacher and has lived and worked in the North of England, Switzerland and Sussex. She is married, with a daughter, son and two grandchildren. Rose began writing when she retired from teaching and found it to be absorbing and creative to study and write. She has had several articles, short stories and poems published and won prizes in competitions for both her poems and short stories. She uses stories from her island past, and also from walking by the sea, which is one of her pleasures.

Anne Callaghan

Anne Callaghan completed a 2 year part-time Creative Writing Programme at the University of Sussex and a course in Dramatic Writing run by New Writing South. She has written poetry, prose, short stories and a novel. After a variety of jobs, including taxi driving and being a security guard at Gatwick, she now works as an administrator in the NHS.

Caroline Collingridge

Caroline Collingridge is a concert flautist, educator and creative arts therapist. She specialised in researching historical women composers and performed and lectured on Women in Music in Europe. She has been writing poems and short stories for many years and lately has included artworks such as etching, linocut and painting. In 2021, she moved to Plymouth in Devon. She is an avid sea swimmer and loves writing about the landscape. She became a volunteer for the Marine Conservation Society to promote the restoration of kelp forests in Sussex and seagrass meadows in Plymouth Sound, the UK's first National Marine Park.

Suzanne Conboy-Hill

A past psychologist, present writer, trainee picture painter, and augmented reality video artist, Suzanne's publications include *Fat Mo*, *Let Me Tell You a Story*, and *Not Being First Fish*. She was a finalist in Best of the Net 2014 with *Puddles Like Pillows*, published by Zouch Magazine and Lascaux literary journal, and has two new collections in the making. Website: conboyhill.com

Paul Doran

Paul should spend more time writing 'cos he really enjoys it, but other things have of late been getting in the way. He's a bit of a news junkie and when inspired it's often about present day social and moral issues, so he's very pleased that reviewing his work for this Anthology has re-enthused him.

Anne Dryden

Anne Dryden is a wife, mother and dog lover. A retired project manager, she returned to full-time education in her fifties, attaining a BA in English and Creative Writing at the University of Chichester in 2017, followed by an MA in Creative and Critical Writing at Sussex in 2019. She spends as much time as possible touring the UK in a motorhome with her husband and their springer spaniel, Daisy. She is currently conducting research into her Somerset mining heritage with a view to perhaps writing a historical novel one day.

Liz Eastwood

Liz Eastwood is a performance poet, plays in a band and runs. Her husband Derek supports with voices off and music. Liz writes social realism and political commentary. She is the self-professed Sestina Queen of the South. Her poetry and prose have been published in numerous anthologies. Liz has been short- and long-listed for the Bridport Prize every year since 2015. She has headlined at venues such as Coast Worthing, Cellar Arts World of Mouth and Tomfoolery and has been on the bill at pubs and clubs in Brighton. She is working on a chap book and her first poetry collection.

Patricia Feinberg Stoner

Patricia Feinberg Stoner is a British writer, author of the *Pays d'Oc* series: *At Home, Tales* and the forthcoming *Murder*. She has also published three books of comic verse. A Londoner by birth, she and her husband spent four years living in the South of France before settling happily on the south coast of England.

Bill Garrod

Bill Garrod spent his entire life from leaving school to retirement working in science based jobs. Firstly, in research projects, to be followed by thirty five years in the medical industry, with jobs ranging from sales rep to MD. He has been married for fifty seven years with two children and two grandchildren. His hobby for many years was sailing, and he finally put pen to paper aged seventy-one with his first novel. This was followed by ten more, none of which have yet been published. "Lost at Sea" is Bill's first short story.

Theresa Gooda

Theresa Gooda's poetry has been published by the Cannon's Mouth, Sentinel Quarterly, the Writer's Bureau English in Education, FMN and the South Downs Poetry Festival. She is the ghostwriter of a series of books about foster carer Louise Allen (Trinity Mirror/Welbeck Publishing), with the seventh, *Max and Mia's Story*, due for publication in April 2023. *Eden's Story* reached the Sunday Times Top Ten bestsellers in February 2021.

Jackie Harvey

Jackie has been a Member of WSW since the late 1990s and served as Secretary on the Committee for several years. She writes flash fiction, short stories, articles and the occasional poem. She has had success in anthologies, magazines and competitions. As well as WSW, Jackie also belongs to a small group of writers at Portslade Library, meeting each month to share work and support.

Mary Jones

Dr Mary Jones has been a teacher and a naval historian. She has published one book and written two unpublished ones. She has published articles and given talks. Her website, Persona Naval Press, still receives relevant information from interested readers.

Mary's life has not been all academic; she spent much time enjoying global travel, and enjoyed raising a family. Sadly, over the years she lost two precious husbands and a dear son to terminal illness, but she now has five surviving children, grandchildren and great grandchildren.

Mary wrote poetry when life became difficult. She plans to write more as she looks to the happy and enjoyable years left. She loves "stream of consciousness stuff", the amazing technique that unravels life for us, "what's it all about Alfie?"

She adheres to Burns' sentiment: "Grow old along o' me, the best is yet to be . . . !"

Alan Lawrie

Having lived in Denmark for 14 years, France for 3 and wth customers all over the world, Alan is a European first, Englishman second, who has spent a career marketing music in Europe but is now happily retired living with his wife, Jacquie, in Worthing, West Sussex writing and publishing books.

His current project is a book about British humour and the quirky world we live in. Future projects include a book about motivational therapy and a sci-fi novel about animal cloning. All of which sounds very grand, but it's not about money, he says but it's fun to write, therapy in semi-retirement, and if he ever sells enough books to keep him in coffee and doughnuts for a year he will be blissfully satisfied.

He and Jacquie self publish through their own Pinky Blue Publishing, with its own website and the ultimate challenge of marketing the books and making them discoverable.

Audrey Lee

Audrey has written bits and pieces all her life: poems, stories and books that started and did not get finished. Having not much belief that she would ever get published, she had a book of short stories printed by a local printer called *Stories From the Plutonian Shore,* which she illustrated with her own paintings and drawings. She then self-published a book of short stories on Amazon called *Flesh and Metal*. It turned out that the whole world had already bagged that title, so if trying to track it down you have to type her name beside it. Now, she writes as the spirit moves, and it doesn't move that often, but she believes she benefits enormously from her membership of West Sussex Writers.

Lawrence Long

Lawrence Long, a member since 1994, chaired WSW 1997-2000. He was born in London and studied German and French literature in London and Germany. A writer since childhood and published since 1980, his mostly financial-sector career included roles as researcher/writer. He lives in Horsham.

Alex Medwell

Alexander Medwell is a performance poet, song writer and percussionist. His other hobbies include amateur dramatics and painting. Alex works full time as general manager of The Airbrush Company in Lancing, West Sussex.

Sarah Palmer

Sarah Palmer teaches creative writing at GBMet (Northbrook), Evolution Arts and on the University of Brighton Work, Write, Live short courses. In her other life she's Fundraising Manager at the West Sussex charity Turning Tides Homelessness.

Jacqui Rozdoba

Jacqui studied fine art in Winchester and spent most of her life in South East London. She has written poetry and short stories, stuffed papers in drawers, and abandoned others to cyberspace. Recently, she decided to expose her work, to share and learn form others, and found that she was not the sole impostor.

She moved to West Sussex four years ago to be with family and breathe clean air. While enjoying a newly found love of the seashore, she misses the vibrancy and diversity of London. Jacqui has had poems from her Fridge Magnet series published by Ekphrastic Review and TORCH. She is working on "Usignoletto", the fictional memoir of a castrato.

John Rudkin

John Rudkin is from Leicestershire. His involvement in writing came from composing comedy songs, which he used to perform with his wife. It was Linda who persuaded him to sign with the East Midlands Writing School and other courses locally after one these was recorded by Robin Laing, the professional Scottish folk singer.

Linda sadly passed away in 2016 and the following year John moved to Worthing to live with his daughter, Rachel, and her husband. He continued with courses at the MET, firstly with Sue Walker, then Sarah Higbee, and now with Sarah Palmer.

Roger Shadbolt

Following a career in the Financial Services Industry, Roger started writing short stories instead of tax guides. He has also had a children's book published and makes the occasional foray into poetry, although he tends to find this the most difficult to write.

Liz Tait

Liz Tait lives in Worthing and writes predominantly for the stage.Her latest all-female ensemble play*Who Do You Think You Are?*was chosen from over 200 new plays to feature in Pleasance's 2019 "Reading Week" in collaboration with Sheer Drop Theatre. They are currently exploring co-production and venue avenues for a tour next year. Previous work includes three plays for Brighton-based theatre Beside the Seaside Productions. These received Brighton Fringe productions, earning five-star reviews and awards including the Fringe Review Award for "Outstanding Theatre" and an Argus Angel award. Liz has recently started trying her hand at writing Flash Fiction.

Cherrie Taylor

Cherrie Taylor lives in West Sussex, where the coast and seashore are important parts of her life. She was told that some of her first words were written in the sand! She has enjoyed writing stories and poetry since childhood. In 2012, she studied Creative Writing with the Open University. She has won prizes for her poetry and short stories. Her work has been published in UK magazines and anthologies. She is an active member of local poetry and creative writing groups. Her debut poetry collection is *Stepping on Shadows* (Dempsey & Windle, 2021). Cherrie's website: https://cherrie84.wixsite.com/website

Fran Tristram

Fran began an online creative writing course during the pandemic. She didn't know whether she would find anything to write about and certainly never imagined that she would be drawn to poetry, never having been much exposed to it nor taken much interest in it before. She found to her surprise and delight that she loved the craft of it, the learning and the process. A little like learning another language, it seemed to open an unfamiliar window, lighting dusty unexplored boxes in her brain.

Michael Wearing

Michael Wearing is a producer, screenwriter and public speaker who relies heavily on his experiences in his 30-year roller-coaster career as a policeman in London's Metropolitan Police. His work includes training films for the police, NHS and local authorities. Michael joined West Sussex Writers to learn about the vast range of writing genres. He is currently rewriting his autobiography and has started work on his first novel.